Strictly Dandia

Sudha Bhuchar and Kristine Landon-Smith

T0262504

Methuen Drama

Published by Methuen Drama 2004

1 3 5 7 9 10 8 6 4 2

First published in 2004 by
Methuen Publishing Limited

A CIP catalogue record for this book is available from the British Library

ISBN 0 413 77422 8

Typeset by Country Setting, Kingsdown, Kent

Tamasha Theatre Company and
the Lyric Hammersmith present

Strictly Dandia

written by Sudha Bhuchar and Kristine Landon-Smith

�֍ BANK OF SCOTLAND

Arts & Business
NEW PARTNERS

This play was first performed at The Kings Theatre, Edinburgh as part of the Edinburgh International Festival on Wednesday 27 August 2003 with the following cast members:

Prema Datani	Sudha Bhuchar
Shanti Patel	Charubala Chokshi
Roopa	Susan Cruse
Pushpa Shah / Hina Shah	Rina Fatania
Mohan Patel / Popatlal Shah	Shiv Grewal
Sonya Patel	Davina Hemlall
Dinesh	Divian Ladwa
Jaz / Bharat Shah	Chris Ryman
Anant	Rehan Sheikh
Shrenek Patel	Sonit Shringi
Raza	Paul Tilley
Preethi	Fiona Wade

This play text is from the original Edinburgh International Festival production; subsequent edits are not included.

Cast

Prema Datani	Sudha Bhuchar
Shanti Patel	Charubala Chokshi
Roopa	Susan Cruse
Pushpa Shah	Shaheen Khan
Hina Shah	Jalpa Patel
Mohan Patel / Popatlal Shah	Shiv Grewal
Sonya Patel	Davina Hemlall
Dinesh	Divian Ladwa
Jaz	Don Klass
Bharat Shah	Simon Nagra
Anant / Ketan	Prashant Kapoor
Shrenek Patel	Sonit Shringi
Raza	Paul Tilley
Preethi	Fiona Wade

Director	Kristine Landon-Smith
Designer	Sue Mayes
Choreographer	Liam Steel
Lighting Designer	Chris Davey
Composer	Shri (Shrikanth Sriram)
Sound Designer	Mike Furness
Sound Operator	Al Ashford
Dramaturge	Graham Devlin
Costume Supervisor	Hilary Lewis
Production Manager	Jo Peake
Company Stage Manager	Lisa Buckley / Kathy Anders
Deputy Stage Manager	Lorna Seymour
Wardrobe Mistress	Helen Johnson
Trainee Director	Samina Baig
Assistant Designer	Rachana Jadhav

With thanks to

Suman Bhuchar, Navin Bhuptani, Jesse Fleck, Mala Ghedia, Mina Jasani, Ashvin-Kumar Joshi, Nicholas Khan, Natasha Mistry, Kiran and Sadhana Patel, Panna, Pal Prasad, John Prescott, Ritish Shah, Satish Shah, San Shella, Stephanie Street, Ramesh Vala OBE, Hardish Virk.

Garbas, Dandias and Bhangras

Most Asians, especially those who feel an attachment to India, don't find Morris dancing absurd. Flushed and hot Englishmen in blouses, bells and brightly coloured bands, waving sticks and jumping in rhythm, playing out memory and ancient ritual, is, as Sanjeev Bhaskar would say on *Goodness Gracious Me*, 'plainly Indian' and a very excellent thing. All human beings need tribal songs and boogie, spaces for collective traditions, the marking of cyclical time. Even more so today when our world seems to be driven by the cults of perfectionism and professionalism, underpinned by ruthless materialism, policed by sneering post-modern snobs who despise anything that appears laughably old-fashioned or amateurish. Asians have never taken any notice of such style-fascists. In fact, like the jitterbugging Caribbeans, they found sustenance, kept their souls uplifted, dancing their old garbas, dandias and bhangras to folksy songs which had come down the centuries. Communal dance helped them cope with the loss of homelands and the indignity of arriving in a place where they were needed but not wanted. Festivals and customs were replanted on this soil so that there was a proper context for the dance. Much of this happened behind closed doors, in garages or backs of shops so the natives would not complain as they watched *Coronation Street*.

Bhangra – a Punjabi village jig – is now well enough known across the tribes of this nation, popularised by films such as *Bend It Like Beckham* and *Monsoon Wedding*. At wedding celebrations – especially of interracial marriages – you commonly see enthusiastic white councillors, Tory ladies or Armani city slickers thumping heavily to the beats of bhangra, freely pointing their forefingers upwards as they shake their bums. The dance has become a powerful metaphor for sexy, irresistible, diverse new Britain.

But the garba and dandia are less well known, perhaps because they have been imported by Gujaratis, who tend to be (and this is a stereotype promoted by Hindu Britons themselves) less brassy and boisterous than Punjabis. Both are circle dances, one using claps the other sticks, repetitively, never deviating much from conventional formats. Garba was mainly for women and dandia for men or both sexes. In East Africa, where so many British Gujaratis come from, garbas and dandias were central to their religious identity. Navratri, nine nights of garba before Diwali marked the defeat of the monstrous Ravan, avowed enemy of Ram and Sita in the battle of Lanka. Navratri, then, was strictly for Hindu women. Asian women were felt for ever to be under threat, vulnerable before the brutish, lascivious black men or wicked, predatory, non-Hindu males. This mild, hospitable community turned hyper-paranoid during Navratri. Hindu men watched out for interlopers – untouchables or Muslim men – and ensured black servants didn't linger to watch the young women. Brawls were commonplace. As ever, it was men guarding female virtue, and creating hell. For the women the circle was more than a protective enclave. The rotating display of Hindu femininity was keenly observed by families looking for brides, a godsend for the unfortunate fathers of too many daughters. Many times over the course of Navratri young, virgin women would fall into a swoon, and have strange hysterics which they later claimed was a divine manifestation. The power, the intoxicating rhythm of dandias and garbas for hours on end, may have released unfamiliar desires and energies to cause these dramatic fits.

These days young British Gujarati men and women – among the most successful groups in this country – are bringing some new dash and daring to Navratri. They hit the sticks harder; there is a new unpredictability to the movements and the mood, although they remain deeply traditional. They now choose their own marriage partners, and these dandia events are safe meeting places for Hindu men and women. This is a showcase for their pride, wealth and increasing self-belief that they are the best, most worthy and obliging, least troublesome immigrants to come to this country after the Second World War.

In some ways Gujarati Hindus are more profoundly English than Caribbeans ever were. They are brilliant small businessmen; they love discretion, dislike too much clamour for rights, accept the establishment and class order (it links in nicely with caste hierarchies) prefer infiltration to revolution, excel at compromises, like to believe they are very tolerant and self-effacing.

These very British Hindus believe they are open people, and everybody is welcome to their festivities. Sudha Bhuchar was frequently told this when she was researching this piece. And yet behind the welcome is steely resolve to keep things controlled and absolute; security at the door (Nigerian bouncers these days) makes sure not too many 'slims' – Muslims – get in to eye the girls. Their own suburban legends tell of rapes when Muslims were allowed in somewhere, some time long ago.

Hindu girls are allowed more independence than Muslim and Sikh girls, but yet, even now, most marry within caste, race and class. A new speed-dating service for just such specificities has been set up recently. And it is here, within the world of modern dandia – more open and unapologetic, yet still a closed circle, that *Strictly Dandia* is set, a personal tale of defiance versus conformity.

Like everything else Tamasha does, this piece is unsettling. To tell the untold is always a risk. To use, as Tamasha always does, an individual tale to wider purpose is more dangerous still, especially with themes like immigration, settlement, cultural battles. How can you do this without didactics and homilies and the argument (used against *East is East*) that the events simply could not happen in good Asian lives? Through beguiling drama, cheek, damn good jokes and an understanding of the intimate moments of big histories. The rising smoke of the kitchen in the unforgettable *Balti Kings* disseminated the pain and strength of immigrants better than any overfunded government report. Tamasha were last in Edinburgh on the festival's fiftieth birthday, presenting *A Tainted Dawn*, stories to mark fifty years from the violent birth of Pakistan. This time the challenge is to 'progressive' Gujarati Hindus who are as prone today to fears of pollution and cultural arrogance as are so many Muslims, Christians and Jews. In some British Hindu temples India is being reclaimed from 'outsiders' – including the people who gave India the Taj Mahal and excuses are made for the murder of over five thousand Muslims in Gujarat. Animosity is growing between young 'infidel idol-worshippers' and 'fundamentalist Muslims' in this country. The love story between Muslim and Hindu Britons, at the heart of *Strictly Dandia*, takes on new meaning and urgent resonance.

Participative dance spaces right from *Romeo and Juliet* are theatres of personal passion where the forces of conservatism – form, pattern, rules, expectations – can be subverted, reconfigured. In the most controlled of societies – Venice in the sixteenth century, Delhi during the Mogul then British rule – dancers used their eyes and feet to challenge throttling norms.

Dance – conventional and iconoclastic – is centre stage in this production; it gives the story further power, and immediacy. The circles of dandia get broken, re-routed and strangers join in, enticing good Hindu girls. Who knows where that will lead? Hopefully to light, more open spaces, which are truly free and welcoming.

Glossary

AMG	Top-of-the-range Mercedes with all the accessories
Auo Jo	'See you soon'
Bhangra	Traditional Punjabi dance, which has been appropriated in Britain
Bhen	Literally 'sister' but used in general among women
Biryani	A rice dish, traditionally made from lamb and rice
Chana Bateta	Chickpea and potato dish
China Whites	Night club in central London
CK	Calvin Klein
Daal	Lentil dish
Diwali	The Hindu 'festival of lights'
Gujus	Colloquial for the Gujaratis
Halo	'Let's go'
Hindu Punjabi	A Hindu person who originates from the region of Punjab in India
Eid	Muslim festival at the end of the month of Ramadan
Karishma Kapoor	Famous Bollywood actress
Krishna	Hindu God
Kutch Kutch hota hai	Bollywood film, shown in mainstream British cinemas
Louis	Lohanna, one of the three castes
Patel	One of the three castes
Pukka	'Great'
Radha	Krishna's consort
Ritek Roshan	Famous Bollywood actor
Roti	Indian bread
Shahs	One of the three castes
Slims	Short for 'Muslim' and often used in a derogatory manner
Uni	University

The Company

Sudha Bhuchar *Prema Datani*
Sudha is joint founder and Artistic Director of Tamasha Theatre Company. She is both an actor and a playwright. She writes regularly with Shaheen Khan for BBC4, and their many credits include three series of *Girlies*. They are currently under commission to BBC Northern Ireland, developing a new six part series. Their screenplay, *The House across the Street*, has recently been shown on BBC 4. Her writing credits for Tamasha include the award-winning *Fourteen Songs, Two Weddings and a Funeral*, *A Tainted Dawn* and the hugely successful *Balti Kings*. Her acting credits include *Murder* by Abi Morgan (BBC), *EastEnders* (BBC), and *Haroun and the Sea of Stories* (Royal National Theatre).

Charubala Chokshi *Shanti Patel*
Charubala had worked for twenty years in film and with the Indian National Theatre in Bombay before starting her acting career in the UK in 1968. Charubala has been in various theatre productions, including *Kirti Sona and Ba* at Leicester Haymarket, *Untouchable* at Riverside Studios and *House of the Sun* at Theatre Royal Stratford East. Charubala has worked on a number of shows for BBC Radio 4 including *Citizens, Women of the Dust, Lizpeth, Beyond the Pale, Pankhiraj* and also *Pravina's Wedding* on Capital Radio. Charubala's television credits include *Casualty, Gems, The Bill, Angels, Blood Red Roses, Romance Romance, Dear Manju, You and Me, Love Match, Pravina's Wedding, Lake of Darkness, Specials, Porterhouse Blue, Moving Story, Between the Lines* and *Story Store*. Charubala also has numerous film credits including *A Fish Called Wanda, My Beautiful Launderette, Gandhi* and *Heirs and Graces*.

Susan Cruse *Roopa*
Since studying acting for TV, film and theatre at Arts International drama school in North Yorkshire Susan started her career in two plays directed by Toby Swift. She played La Braukmann in *Conquest of the South Pole* and Mrs Martin in Ionesco's *Bald Prima Donna*. Susan's younger roles have included Dorothy in *The Wizard of Oz* directed by John Sichel, who also cast her as Marie-Louise in *My Three Angels*. Recently Susan played Hermia in *A Midsummer Night's Dream*, Evelyn in *Absent Friends* at the Questors Theatre and Liat in *South Pacific*.

Chris Davey *Lighting Designer*
For Tamasha Chris has designed *Balti Kings, Fourteen Songs Two Weddings and a Funeral* and *Ghostdancing*. Designs in opera include *Jephtha* (Welsh National Opera), three seasons at Grange Park Opera, *The Picture of Dorian Gray* (Opera de Monte Carlo), *La Traviata* for Castleward Opera Belfast, *Gli Equivoci Nel Sebiant* for Batignano Opera, Tuscany. For the Royal Shakespeare Company: *Cymbeline, Night of the Soul, Romeo and Juliet, A Midsummer Night's Dream, Everyman* (both also in New York), *A Month in the Country, The Comedy of Errors* (world tour). Chris has designed extensively for Shared Experience Theatre, West Yorkshire Playhouse, Royal Exchange Manchester, Royal Lyceum Theatre Edinburgh, Theatre Royal Stratford East. Chris's recent designs include, *21* (Rambert Dance Company), *Crazyblackmuthaf***ingself* and *Sugar Syndrome* (Royal Court), *Romeo and Juliet* (Chichester Festival Theatre), *The Vagina Monologues* (national tour), *My One and Only* (Piccadilly Theatre and Chichester), *Dangerous Corner* (Garrick Theatre), *Jekyll and Hyde* (Northern Ballet Theatre), *The Car Man* Adventures in Motion Pictures (Winner of Best Musical Event Evening Standard Awards), *Honk!* (national tour), *Closer* (Abbey Theatre Dublin), *Baby Doll* (Albery Theatre, Royal National Theatre, Birmingham Rep), *Shining Souls* (Old Vic), *In a Little World of Our Own, Endgame* (Donmar Warehouse), *Blood Wedding, Grimm Tales* (Young Vic) and *Madame Bovary* (Lyric Hammersmith for Shared Experience Theatre).

Graham Devlin *Dramaturge*
From 1973-1997, Graham Devlin was Artistic Director of Major Road, directing more than 70 productions for the company, several of which he wrote. Productions included *Mohicans* (also for television), *Irish Night, The Bottle Imp* and *Jekyll and Hyde*. He has also worked extensively as a freelance director in the United Kingdom and abroad. Latterly, much of this work has been in the field of music-theatre, where he has worked for, among others, Scottish Opera, the Aldeburgh Festival, Glyndebourne Education Department and on the Contemporary Music Network. In 1987, Devlin was invited by Sir Harrison Birtwistle to join the National Theatre in order to direct two Birtwistle pieces – *Down by the Greenwood Side* and *Bow Down*. This collaboration continued in 1991 with Devlin's production of the composer's *Punch and Judy* at the Aldeburgh Festival, in Vienna and in Berlin. Other stage work has included Adrian Henri's version of *The Wakefield Mysteries* at Pontefract Castle, *Under African Skies* for Adzido Pan-African Dance Ensemble and

the opera *Poe* at Sydney Opera House, for which he wrote the libretto to Andrew Ford's music. His second operatic collaboration with Ford, *The World Knot*, was also produced in Australia while his cantata *Out of the Darkness* with music by Paul Robinson was premiered by Northern Sinfonia. After leaving Major Road, Graham Devlin served as Deputy Secretary General and Acting Chief Executive of the Arts Council of England.

Mike Furness *Sound Designer*
Theatre designs include: *All's Well That Ends Well* and *As You Like It* (RSC at the Barbican). *Blues in the Night*, *The Witches*, *Ladyday*, *The BFG* (West End). He has also designed for the Kings Head, the Tricycle, Paines Plough, the New Vic, as well as numerous shows for the Brighton and Edinburgh Festivals. He has produced audio drama for the Natural History Museum .The majority of his work is designing sound systems for concert, corporate, and other live events worldwide. This is his sixth sound design for Tamasha.

Shiv Grewal *Mohan Patel / Popatlal Shah*
Shiv has worked extensively with Tamasha on stage, as well as radio and film. He last appeared in *Fourteen Songs, Two Weddings and a Funeral*, and prior to that in *Balti Kings* at the West Yorkshire Playhouse. Shiv has numerous theatre, radio and television credits and can be heard in the BBC World Service soap *Westway*. On television he has been on the Channel 4 drama *Second Generation* and the Jack Rosental drama *When You Are Ready Mr McGill*. Although no stranger to film, he is currently busy behind the camera writing and animating.

Davina Hemlall *Sonya Patel*
Davina graduated from East 15 acting school last year. Her recent television credits include the role of Parminder in *Second Generation* and a commercial for Seeboard Energy. Since graduating she has worked with Ken Campbell as a Gastromancer at both the Commonwealth Institute and the Angel Puppet Theatre. She has also appeared in many variety shows at the Theatre Royal in Stratford. Previous achievements include being a cheerleader for West Ham football club, winning two gold medals in an international dance competition in Euro Disney, Paris, and doing *Blues Brothers* and *Fame* at the Queens Theatre in Hornchurch. She has played a variety of roles, such as Varya in *The Cherry Orchard*, Mrs Figgup in *The Virtuoso*, Galina in *Brezhnev's Children*, Messua in *The Jungle Book*, Estelle in *Nana* and various roles in *Oh! What a Lovely War* and most recently *Thumbelina* at the Steven Joseph Theatre.

Prashant Kapoor *Anant / Ketan*
Prashant trained in drama at the New York Film Academy and the Mountview Academy in London and was coached in Indian theatre by Satya Dev Dubey. He has appeared as Shiva in *Colour* at the South Bank Centre, directed by Surya Kumari, Manav in *Misogynist and the Alcoholic*, Akshay in *May I Ask a Question?* directed by Satya Dev Dubey, Champu's husband in *Sakharam Binder*, directed by Shyamanand, Vijay in *Desh Mein Nikla Hoga Chand*, directed by Aroona Irani for Star Plus TV, and Richard Bach in *The Journey* (NYFA Films). He is Head of Bollywood Dance at the Padmini Kolhapure School of Dancing, London, and has taught Bollywood Film Dance for the past ten years. He choreographed for the Bollywood film *Dil Aashiquana Hai* and was assistant choreographer for films such as *Rajkumar*, *Paanch* and *Khullam Khulla Pyar Karengay*. He also appeared in *Bollywood Queen*, directed by Jeremy Wooding. Prashant studied Law (LLB) at the London School of Economics and Political Science, and worked as a solicitor for an international law firm. He is currently writing a novel which will be coming out later this year, and is the author of *Change Your Life – Feng Shui* (Rupa Publications, India, 2003).

Shaheen Khan *Pushpa Shah*
Shaheen's theatre credits include *Invisible Kids* (Contact Theatre), *Borderline* (Nuffield Theatre), *Kirti, Sona and Ba* (Leicester Haymarket), *A Tainted Dawn* and *House of the Sun* (Tamasha Theatre), *The Little Clay Cart* (Arts Theatre), *Midnight's Children* (RSC). Her television credits include for the BBC *Love Match*, *Love Birds*, *Old Flame*, *My Sister Wife*, *Not Even God is Wise Enough*, *Flight*, *Man of the Month*, *Parosi-Neighbours*, *Casualty*, *Holby City* and *Grange Hill*; for ITV *The Bill*, and *Family Pride* and *Tandoori Nights* for Channel 4. Films include *Partition*, *Sammy and Rosie Get Laid*, *Hollow Reed*, *Captives*, *Tomorrow Never Dies*, *Bhaji on the Beach* and *Bend it Like Beckham*. Shaheen writes regularly with Sudha Bhuchar, and their collaborations for Radio 4 include *Girlies* (three series, shortlisted for CRE award) and the *Dancing Girls of Lahore*; for theatre *Balti Kings*; and for television *The House Across the Street* (BBC4) and *Doctors* (BBC1). They are currently developing an idea for BBC Northern Ireland for a six part series.

Don Klass *Jaz*

Don trained in Musical Theatre and Drama at the Sylvia Young Theatre School. His talents as an actor have brought him success in theatre productions including; *Monkey* (The Young Vic), *A Midsummer Night's Dream* (Palace Theatre, Redditch), *The Jungle Book* (Haymarket Theatre, Basingstoke), *Oliver* (The London Palladium) and *Five Buddies in a Box* (The Savoy). Don has appeared in numerous commercials, films and television programmes such as *The Web, Casualty, The Bill, Fight School, Legal Tender, Gadabout* and *The Barrymore Show*, as well as being a skilled voice-over artist, recording the BBC Radio play *Feathers* and appearing on *Newsround*. Don is also a talented dancer and musician and is highly skilled in martial arts. He was the National Wu Shu Champion in 2001, holds the combat Wu Shu Championship and holds a Black Belt in Karate.

Divian Ladwa *Dinesh*

Divian studied at The City Lit doing a variety of professional courses in drama, dance and singing. He made his first stage debut as a dancer with Rambert's 'Centre Stage'. After this he devised his own play based on the political figure William Wilberforce, integrating drama, dance and music. Since appearing with Tamasha at the Edinburgh International Festival, Divian has been working with Nick Pattachio's Imagination Films. He featured in Wing Kit Looi's film *Tomorrow*, for which he also choreographed the fight sequence. His affiliation with the Precinct Theatre, his studies and experiences so far have inspired him to take up playwriting.

Kristine Landon-Smith *Director*

Kristine is joint founder and Artistic Director of Tamasha and has also directed all of the company's shows. Her 1996 production, *East is East*, was nominated for an Olivier award and her original production of *Fourteen Songs, Two Weddings and a Funeral* won the Barclays Theatre Award for Best New Musical. Her work for BBC Radio has included many productions of which *A Yearning* and *Women of the Dust* won CRE Race in the Media Awards. Other freelance directing work has been with the Royal Court Theatre, Bristol Old Vic, Palace Theatre Westcliff and Nitro. She has most recently been producing for the World Service Soap *Westway*.

Sue Mayes Designer

Sue trained at Central School of Art and Design (Central St Martins) in the 1970s and has designed all of Tamasha's shows. Her career started with residencies at Ipswich Rep, the Belgrade Theatre and the Liverpool Everyman, and her other freelance work has included designs for Royal Shakespeare Company, Talawa Theatre Company, Bristol Old Vic, Theatre Royal Stratford East and the Southwark Playhouse. She is particularly interested in visual theatre and cultural research based design. She teaches regularly at drama schools across London, including the Central School of Speech and Drama and Guildhall School of Music and Drama.

Simon Nagra Bharat

Simon's recent theatre productions include the RSC's *Antony and Cleopatra* (Duke's Playhouse Lancaster), *Arabian Nights*, a UK and Bosnia Herzegovina tour of *Crime of the 21st Century*, a new play by Edward Bond and Yellow Earth's *Play to Win* (UK tour & Soho Theatre). He appeared in *Hiawatha* at the Haymarket Theatre, Basingstoke, and in the National Theatre's production of Salman Rushdie's *Haroun and the Sea of Stories*. Other productions include *East* for Snarling Beasties, *Cultivated Wilderness* for Spectacle Theatre, *Embryo of Death* for The Young Vic, *A Song for a Sanctuary* at the Lyric Hammersmith, Cominius and Aufidius in *Coriolanus*, D'Labardamount in *The Devils* and Schmitz in *The Fire Raisers*, all for the Duke's Playhouse, Lancaster. He has also appeared in *End of Season* for Red Ladder, *A Tainted Dawn, Ghostdancing* and *East is East* for Tamasha Theatre Company, *Kahinni* for Birmingham Rep and Asaph Chawn in *Aureng-Zebe* at the National Theatre Studio. His radio work includes *A New Life, Dreams of Tipu Sultan, Shoulders, Voices on the Wind, Come to Mecca, Saving Grace, Hillcrest, Dancing Girls of Lahore, Guess Who's coming to Christmas* and *The Archers* for Radio 4, and *Bounty Hunters* for Radio 5. On television he has been seen in *The Bill, Casualty* and *EastEnders*. Further work includes *Home, Popcorn* and *Grease Monkeys* for the BBC. Later in the year he can be seen in *Down to Earth* for the BBC and *The Last Detective* for Granada. He also appeared in the short film *Midnight Feast* for Tamasha Films.

Jalpa Patel *Hina Shah*

Jalpa has studied drama since the age of eleven at the Harris Drama School. She has also studied classical Indian dance from a very young age and recently performed her Arangetram, Indian dance graduation show. Professionally, Jalpa appeared as the regular character of Anika in *Grange Hill* for a very successful four-year run. This production marks her professional theatrical debut.

Sonit Shringi *Shrenek Patel*
Whilst studying Sonit acted in various roles at College: Riff in *West Side Story*, Tevye in *Fiddler on the Roof*, Frizzy and O'Leary in *Bugsy Malone*. Sonit's debut was in 2000 in the fringe award-winning play *BBA and Proud*, in which he played the lead. The show then went on to perform a national tour including theatres such as Bristol Old Vic and Lyric Hammersmith. TV credits include various voiceovers for Channel 4 during their Indian Summer Season and performances in *Buddha of Suburbia* and *Grange Hill*. He has also conducted several workshops in schools to help with voice and movement Skills.

Shri (Shrikanth Sriram) *Composer*
Multi-instrumentalist, composer, and producer Shrikanth Sriram was brought up in Bombay, India, where he trained as a classical tabla player before developing a taste for jazz and learning the bass guitar. Now UK-based since 1997, he has released three albums under Outcaste Records, *Drum the Bass* in 1997 and, in collaboration with DJ Badmarsh, *Dancing Drums* in 1998 and *Signs* in 2001. His diverse experiences are reflected in his compositions, rolling drum'n'bass, sublime filmic trances and funky grooves, which travel the length and breadth of deepest India to deepest South London. His composition work in theatre/dance has included *Alladeen* with Moti Roti and The Builders Association (New York) and *Coming of Age* directed by Keith Khan at the South Bank.

Liam Steel *Choreographer*
Liam works as a performer, director and choreographer. For eight years he was a core member of DV8 Physical Theatre as both a performer and Assistant/Associate Director of the company. Productions included *MSM*; *Enter Achilles* (including the award-winning film version); *Bound to Please*; *The Happiest Day of My Life*; and *The Cost of Living*. Other performance credits include work with Nottingham Playhouse; the Royal Court; Manchester Royal Exchange; the Kosh; Volcano Theatre Co; Roundabout Theatre Co; Gay Sweatshop; Theatr Powys; Footloose Dance Company (Powys Dance); Nigel Charnock and Company; Theatre Centre; Frantic Assembly; Royal National Theatre Studio; Graeae Theatre Co; Theatre de Complicite and David Glass Ensemble. Recent directorial/choreographic work includes *Pericles* (RSC/Cardboard Citizens Theatre Co); *Devotion* (Theatre Centre); *Frankenstein* (Blue Eyed Soul Dance Company); *Heavenly* (Frantic Assembly/Soho Theatre); *Vurt* (Contact Theatre Manchester); *The Fall of the House of Usher* (Graeae Theatre Co); *Look at Me* (Theatre Centre); *Hymns* (Lyric Hammersmith/Frantic Assembly); *Sparkleshark* (Royal National Theatre); *The Flight* (Restless Dance Co, Adelaide Festival, Australia); *15 Degrees and Rising* (Circus Space); *The Secret Garden*, *Beauty and the Beast*, *Tom's Midnight Garden* (Library Theatre, Manchester).

Paul Tilley *Raza*
Paul Tilley was born and raised in London and studied for three years at Laine Theatre Arts School. He has appeared in a number of productions including *The Pied Pier of Hamlin*, *The Crucible*, *My Fair Lady*, *Real Lives*, *Forty-Second Street*, *Fame: the Musical*, *Starlight Express*, *An Indian Takes the Bronx*, *The Lion King* and more recently *Bombay Dreams*.

Fiona Wade *Preethi*
Fiona trained at Bodens in Enfield, Middlesex, and has many professional credits behind her. She played Anya in *24 Seven* for Granada Television (two series) and Joanna Day for three years in the popular series *Grange Hill* for BBC Television. Other television work includes *Boot Street Band*, *The Broom Cupboard* and *Live and Kicking* for the BBC, and most recently two episodes of *Doctors*. Theatre credits include Juliet in *Romeo and Juliet* (Palace Theatre. Redditch), Princess Jasmine in *Aladdin* at Theatre Royal Nottingham, with Cannon & Ball, Yasmin in *Inner City Jam* at West Yorkshire Playhouse, Princess in *Aladdin* at Malvern Festival Theatre, Juliet in *Romeo and Juliet* and Maria in *West Side Story* at the Courtyard Theatre, Hereford, the title role in *Cinderella* at Theatre Royal Stratford, and most recently Kim in *Miss Saigon* at Malmo Opera och Musikteater in Sweden.

Tamasha Theatre Company

Tamasha is the British Asian theatre company committed to disclosing the untold stories. We believe in the personal as a way to illuminate the universal in all our lives. Tamasha's performances are inspired by Asian culture and aim to draw the audience into the very heart of the story. A new writing company, we work and research extensively within communities to uncover a rich and diverse range of stories and voices. Our strong visual style evokes an atmospheric beauty, be it in a Birmingham kitchen or a summer festival in the Punjab. As our name suggests, Tamasha aims to 'create a drama' out of the untold stories of people's lives.

Since its founding in 1989, the company has produced eleven new plays, five of which have been adapted for Radio Four and two have won the CRE Award in the Media Awards. The 1996 production *East is East* was nominated for an Olivier Award, won a Writers' Guild Award and was made into the hugely popular British film. The 1998 production *Fourteen Songs, Two Weddings and a Funeral* won both the BBC Asia award for Achievements in the Arts and the Barclays Theatre Award for Best Musical, as well as enjoying a sell-out London run and two national remounts. In 2002, Tamasha's Artistic Directors were listed in the *Guardian* newspaper's top ten producers.

Tamasha Theatre Company
Unit 220, Great Guildford Business Square,
16–48 Great Guildford Street, London SE1 0HS
t. 020 7609 2411   **f.** 020 7609 2722
e. info@tamasha.org.uk   **w.** www.tamasha.org.uk

LYRIC HAMMERSMITH

PLAY YOUR PART

Finally, we would like to thank the following individuals and organisations for supporting our work on stage and in the community in the financial years 2002/3 and 2003/4.

Anonymous
Michael and Joy Alinek
P Allatt
Arts Council England
Association of London Government
Arts & Business New Partners
Mrs A Bartholomew
F Campbell
The Canadian High Commission in Britain
Children's Fund
City Inn
The Ernest Cook Trust
Prudence Downing
Mr R A Dundas
EMI Music UK and Ireland
European Social Fund Objective 3
Esmée Fairbairn Foundation
Roger de Freitas
Gingko Garden Centre
The Girdlers' Company
David and Susan Glass
Goethe Institut Inter Nationes
The Goldsmiths' Company
Government of Quebec
The Paul Hamlyn Foundation
Wendy Hefford
Help a London Child
Heritage Lottery Fund
Gerald Hopkinson

HSBC Bank plc
Ambrosine Hurt
The Ironmongers' Company
Italian Cultural Institute
Mrs F Kenton
Rose Knox-Peebles
Lloyds TSB Foundation for England and Wales
London Borough of Hammersmith & Fulham
London Marriott Hotel Kensington
London West Learning and Skills Council
Lyric Friends
Mr I D Metherell
Michael Philip Michaels
Mr and Mrs F W L Moore
Anne Neville
Adrian Norridge
North Fulham New Deal for Communities
Mr Tony Notley
Ms V Owen
Paragon Hotel
John H Reed
Royal Netherlands Embassy
The Royal Victoria Hall Foundation
Mrs R Vera Salama
Linda Seal
Mhairi Stewart
Sure Start Broadway/Margravine
Sure Start Coningham
A W F Washbourne
Mrs J Wilson
Youth Music

LYRIC HAMMERSMITH

Coming Soon

20 February – 27 March
Lyric Hammersmith

Oliver Twist

Charles Dickens
Adapted and directed by Neil Bartlett
In this powerful new adaptation of Dicken's classic novel, Neil Bartlett
brings back to the theatre one of the angriest, funniest and most deeply
felt stories about childhood ever written.

3 – 4 April

Here Comes Everyone

To coincide with The Catch, our annual celebration of all that is surprising
and original in international children's theatre, music and dance, we're
finally opening our new front door with a free weekend of performances,
installations and happenings ... Bring the family; explore the building;
explore your imagination ...

8 - 24 April
A Cultural Industry Project produced in collaboration
with West Yorkshire Playhouse and the Lyric Hammersmith

Shockheaded Peter

The legend returns to Hammersmith. To celebrate the opening of the
Lyric's new front door, we've reunited The Tiger Lillies and the original
cast for the last ever London performances of the scrumptiously gruesome
and wickedly ghoulish Oliver-award winning junk opera.

Lyric Studio
24 February - 6 March
Stan's Cafe

Good & True/Be Proud of Me

Directed by James Yarker
Stan's Cafe, landing in London for the first time after an acclaimed European
tour, create gripping devised theatre with a comically dark heart.

THE PIONEER OF NEW
WAVE INDIAN RESTAURANTS

CAFE

Lazeez

RESTAURANT AND BAR

Cafe Lazeez is delighted to join Tamasha in
making new waves in British Asian culture

"Cafe Lazeez is perfect" The Sunday Times
"Excellent food" Harpers and Queen

88 St John Street
London
EC1
T: 020 7253 2224

21 Dean Street
London
W1
T: 020 7434 9393

93/95 Old Brompton Road
London
SW7
T: 020 7581 9993

116 Wharfside Street
Birmingham
B1
T: 0121 643 7979

Strictly Dandia

Characters

Prema
Pushpa
Popatlal
Preethi
Roopa
Bharat
Sonya
Shrenek
Jaz
Raza
Shanti
Ketan
Hina
Dinesh
Anant
Mohan

The play is set over one Navratri season in contemporary London.

Scene One

A big gymnasium hall in a leisure centre on the North Circular. Characters enter and sit on the grandstand. **Shrenek** *and* **Sonya** *(young Patels from Tooting, in the competition),* **Pushpa** *and* **Popatlal** *(Shah couple, on the committee),* **Bharat** *and* **Dinesh Shah** *(accountant and IT whizz son) and* **Shanti** *(widow),* **Anant** *(choreographer),* **Preethi Datani** *(pretty young Lohana girl) and* **Roopa** *(her best friend). They wait for the festivities to begin as we hear* **Prema Datani** *on the tannoy.*

Prema *Bhaiyo ne Bheno*, Mayor and Mayoress . . . ladies and gentlemen, boys and girls . . . welcome. This is Prema Datani, your hostess, Chair of Lohana Ladies for last five years. There are so many Navratri celebrations in London but none as famous as the Lohana Ladies. The hall is the same, I know, but that is the only thing. On behalf of my committee, I'm proud to announce an Intercaste dance competition . . . Patels, Lohanas and Shahs, all together competing for the much-coveted titles of Diwali King and Queen. The two lucky winners will be crowned at the grand finale on Saturday. They will have the honour of taking their place on the number-one float at the Diwali parade and switching on the seasonal lights on Ealing Road.

A light isolates **Popatlal** *and* **Pushpa**. *The convention is that when the characters speak, no one else can hear them.*

Puspha Intercaste dance competition! I never heard of such a thing. That Prema Datani is full of progressive ideas. Lohanas. Even the way they look, they are different. Fair-skinned and attitude problem, *he ne*? I don't mind pun the way she looks down on us.

Popatlal We Shahs might be businessy but at least we mind our own business.

Pushpa Every year she gets this hall for the Lohanas, even though Bharat Shah who looks after the tenders is one of us.

Popatlal He is accountant, and Prema's husband Ketan is his biggest client.

Pushpa   If we had this hall even for one year we would do traditional Navratri, respecting the religious significance of the festival.

Popatlal   Well, Bharat knows which side his bread is buttered. It's not surprising he forgets he's a Shah.

Pushpa   The biggest and best hall . . . so central . . . just off the North Circular. I'm going to make sure our daughter dances with Bharat's son. Dinesh is in IT and Hina has done computer course. They have always been close. They surf and talk sometimes . . . in her bedroom. I don't mind as long as door is open. Hina's a good girl. They won the fancy dress as children, *tumhe yaad che*? When I sent Hina as Radha and Dinesh came as Krishna.

Popatlal   Tell the youngsters to make it official then this season.

Pushpa   That's if Bharat agrees. He's got his eyes set on Prema's daughter for his son. As if you can jump caste so easily.

The light now isolates **Preethi** *and* **Roopa**.

Preethi   So you fasting, Roops?

Roopa   Apart from a bar of Snickers.

Preethi   Chocolate counts with God. What happens if you don't fall for a Louis?

Roopa   You get outcast if you marry out of caste.

Preethi   I'd risk it for a Hindu Punjabi.

Roopa   Its true Punjabis are better looking but at least you know when a Gujarati boy is wearing a suit he's paid for it.

Preethi   What about Dinesh? He's a babe-magnet.

Roopa   One, he's a Shah. Two, he's a geek. Those Patels from Tooting are lowering the tone.

The light now isolates **Bharat** *and* **Dinesh Shah**.

Bharat   Preethi Datani is bound to be the Diwali Queen . . .
Prema has been giving her dancing lessons since she was
six . . . Dinesh, *dikro*, you can dance. When your mother
was alive she was always telling you . . . Just need some
confidence. Do your best. Smile . . . Mr Ketan Datani is
a high-net-worth individual and already he is thrilled with
the way you've transformed his stocktaking systems. Gotta
have ambition. When *olo* Idi Amin chucked me out, I came
with just my muffler and anorak, and look where I am
now. If Ketan sees you dancing with his daughter and
winning the Diwali King, who knows, he might be prepared
to forget you are a Shah and then think where it might
lead.

The light now isolates **Sonya** *and* **Shrenek**.

Sonya   These North London Lohana girls. Hasn't anyone
told them that highlights are out?

Shrenek   The guys are worse. How can you wear CK
jeans? South of the river is where the style is.

Sonya   We're the only semi-professionals here. Those
Louyes might be 'full of it' but have they got the range of
moves? The medals that we have? Granby Hall in Leicester,
Birmingham, Wolverhampton.

Shrenek   Amateurs. Weekend dancers with no commit-
ment.

Sonya   I bet none of them go to Pineapple for classes.
Or train with Beni Katania. Our mix of old-school ballet,
jazz and Dandia is gonna proper blow their minds.

Shrenek   They call it a competition when there is no
competition. We might be Patels, but there's no corner-shop
mentality with us.

Sonya   Winning Diwali King and Queen's gonna open
doors for us. You don't think the diamante crown's tempting
fate?

Shrenek   Fate? It's fait accompli, babe . . . we'll walk it.

The garba *begins and one by one they start to dance.*

Prema *(tannoy announcement)*   I just want to remind everyone of the religious significance of our festival. There is a dress code. Save the halter necks and navel jewels for Disco Dandia night. Ladies, make sure your hair is open if your back is bare and make sure your shoulders are covered, otherwise a committee member will ask you to cover up.

As the dance progresses, **Jaz** *and* **Raza** *(two Muslim boys in their twenties) enter. They stand on the sidelines for a while and watch.* **Preethi** *recognises* **Raza**. *They join in the dancing.* **Preethi** *is clearly not happy to see him there. The dance gets faster and we hear* **Prema** *again on the tannoy.*

Prema   Prema Datani again. The judges are going around spotting and short-listing. For those who want to choose their own partner . . . great! But for the singletons, your numbers will be pulled out of a hat. As Hindus, we believe in destiny, so we're going to let Fate choose your dance partners! I hope Fate chooses well. Your dance partner could become your partner for life. The rules are relaxed. Standard steps or stand out! We are not looking for Strictly Dandia!

The dance reaches a crescendo and finishes.

Scene Two

Same night. A little while later. Near the drinks kiosk. In the background three people are texting on their mobile phones. **Jaz** *and* **Raza** *enter.* **Shanti** *is clearing away her kiosk of drinks and confectionery.*

Jaz   That Preethi's stressing with you, man.

Raza   Yeah, it was a prickly exchange. She don't mind meeting at Leicester Square but she doesn't want me here . . . with her family around . . . her community.

Jaz   You knew there was going to be sandpaper between you.

Raza I know, but I had to come and see who they've got lined up for her.

Jaz You gotta get real, Raza. This is the Guju marriage market, and she's gonna pick one of them. Doesn't stop you testing her out and doing an MOT.

Raza We shouldn't have come here.

Jaz Too late. Our numbers were chosen out of the hat. Fate wants you to dance with Preethi . . . and my one's sweet. Her name's Roopa. We've swapped digits . . . She's smitten.

Raza That's 'cos she don't know you're a Muslim.

Jaz She's got a wicked arse.

Raza Grow up, Jaz. Act your age.

Jaz I am acting my age.

Raza These girls are classy women. Don't go talking about her arse in front of her. That's all you see.

Jaz That's 'cos I'm not gay.

Raza I know you're not gay . . . What about personality? Charisma?

Jaz Charisma . . . Karishma Kapoor. She's rough.

Raza *approaches* **Shanti**.

Raza Two Cokes, please.

Shanti (*giving him the Coke*) I've locked the cash tin. You give me one pound tomorrow.

Shanti *looks at* **Raza** *closely and thinks she recognises him.*

Shanti I know you from somewhere. I never forget a face.

Raza (*also recognising her, but not wanting to admit to it*) I don't think so.

Shanti You live in Wembley?

Raza   No.

Shanti   Ah . . . Heathrow Airport!

Jaz   You know people that live in the Airport?

Shanti (*to Raza*)   Your father is that agency fellow, *he ne?*

Raza (*uncomfortable*)   Recruitment consultant.

Shanti   Mr Khan. He got me cleaning job at Heathrow.

Raza   We're not here to cause trouble.

Shanti   I wasn't supposed to work at my age, but your father always said, 'It's work that keeps you alive.' He never told anyone how old I was. I too can keep a secret.

Raza   Thank you.

Shanti   In East Africa we lived side by side. Your people celebrated our Diwali and only because I am vegetarian, I couldn't eat your *biryanis* on the Festival of Idd.

Pushpa, **Popatlal** *and* **Hina** *are leaving, and* **Preethi** *and* **Prema** *are saying goodbye to them.* **Raza** *and* **Jaz** *are also leaving.*

Popatlal   You have done it again, Prema. You Lohana Ladies are one step ahead.

Prema   Well, we like to be the trend-setters.

Pushpa   Half the job is done for you in choice of venue, *he ne?*

Prema   Well, North London is Lohana and Lohana is North London. As soon as the Gujarati calendar comes out, we snap up dates for next year's Navratri.

Pushpa   Well, you know people in the right places, *he ne?*

Popatlal   The Mayor and Mayoress? They are Shahs. I'm surprised you got them as your chief guests.

Prema   Bharat Shah managed to get us in their calendar.

Popatlal   Bharat is very well connected.

Pushpa (*about Raza*)   And this is the boy who has got all the tongues wagging. Is it your friend, Preethi?

Preethi   Yes.

Popatlal   You musn't be too shy to introduce him. That's what these functions are for. Boys and girls meeting and courting. Even our Lord Krishna would dance with his 'girlfriends'.

Prema   Youngsters are all chaperoned. We want them to enjoy and have fun. Better than going behind parents' backs.

Preethi (*to everyone, but keeping a closer eye on Prema's reaction*) This is Raj, and Jaz.

General greeting from everyone.

Pushpa   Raj, lovely to meet you. You are Punjabi?

Raza   Yeah . . . that's right.

Jaz   Punjabi and proud.

Preethi   Raj, this is my mum, Prema, and this is Pushpa aunty and . . .

Popatlal   Popatlal Shah. Everyone calls me PS . . . (*Laughing at his own joke.*) That way I always have the last word. Punjabi . . . Thought I recognised a bit of bhangra there. (*Making a silly gesture of the arms in bhangra.*) A bit of changing the light bulbs . . . Well, Prema, this is the proof in the pudding . . . The success of your 'open door' policy.

Prema   Well, anyone is welcome as long as they respect the intention.

Popatlal   Yes, the only difference between us and Punjabis is they eat *parathas* and we eat *daal bhat*, and it is showing in our bodies, isn't it, Raj?

Raza   Yes.

Pushpa   The trouble starts when the Muslims come in, isn't it?

Prema   We've never had any 'incidents' at our functions.

Popatlal   Well, they can't look at their girls, they come to look at ours, and one of these days it's going to happen the other way round and then what will happen?

Jaz   The Gujus'll get mashed up, innit?

Raza   It's been nice to meet you.

Jaz *and* **Raza** *leave.*

Popatlal   Okay then. *Auo jo.* Maybe next time we get to see your good husband.

Prema   Ketan's very busy.

Pushpa   Oh yes, always busy.

Popatlal   He is busy minting money, ahh . . . He was telling me about your conservatory . . . under-floor heating, ah . . . anything to keep the wives happy? *Halo* . . .

Pushpa   You didn't let me have conservatory.

Popatlal   Where would I put my barbeque?

Pushpa (*to* **Prema**)   Honestly, Prema *bhen* . . . The way these men want to eat meat. I don't mind it outside. I make sure they cook my corn on the cob before they put on their chicken.

Popatlal *and* **Pushpa** *exit.*

Prema   So why you didn't tell me you had a special friend?

Preethi   Mum, he's just a friend?

Prema   From uni?

Preethi   No. I met him outside the sweet shop.

Prema   That's nice. You didn't say? Is he a student?

Preethi   No . . . he's got his own business . . . drives the same car as Dad's.

Ketan *enters.*

Ketan   Ready? I'm expecting an international call.

Preethi   Hi, Dad.

Ketan   How's my baby? Had the boys falling at your feet?

Prema   I hope you're going to use your hands-free because I'm not sitting in the car park while you talk to Dubai.

Ketan   It's these deals that have paid for your conservatory.

Prema   And the bar is for your cocktail parties.

Ketan   Yes, darling.

Prema   And who coped with the builders?

Ketan   You do everything in the house.

Prema   Not just at home, darling. The Mayor and Mayoress were so impressed with my function they've agreed to be the judges on the finale.

Ketan   That's good.

Prema   And you will be coming to that?

Ketan   Of course. Datani Sparks is the sponsor. I'll be bringing some clients.

Prema   Don't forget you're partnering me at the dinner and dance on Tuesday.

Ketan   You better get my dinner jacket dry-cleaned.

Prema   It's already hanging in your cupboard. (*Saying goodbye to* **Shanti**.) *Au jo*, Shant *bhen*. Please make sure everything is cleared away. They have got basketball practice in the hall first thing in the morning.

Shanti   *Auo jo.*

Scene Three

A rehearsal room. Early evening.

Roopa   I'll dance with Jaz if you dance with Raj.

Preethi   I dunno.

Roopa   I thought you said you'd risk it for a Hindu Punjabi.

Preethi   Look, my mum's the chairperson.

Roopa   So you're all mouth?

Preethi   She wasn't that pleased to see that I got partnered with some fella I met outside the sweet shop.

Roopa   You cow, you've been seeing Raj and you never told me. I thought I was your best friend.

Preethi   A girl's gotta have some secrets.

Roopa   Bitch. So how about it? Let's dance with them. There's safety in numbers.

Preethi   Look, I've already texted Raj and told him he can't be my partner.

Roopa   Thanks a million. What am I meant to say to Jaz? He's really keen . . . he's left me five messages.

Preethi   You're on your own.

Roopa   So now I have to find another partner.

Preethi   Join the club.

Roopa   I'm going to get some water. Want anything?

Preethi   No.

Roopa *exits.* **Preethi** *is alone for a moment before* **Jaz** *and* **Raza** *enter.*

Preethi I don't believe this. How did you know I was gonna be here? This is a rehearsal.

Raza I know, and we've got a personal invitation.

Preethi From who?

Jaz Your batty boy friend . . . the Gujarati Wayne Sleep.

Preethi What?

Raza That choreographer geezer . . .

Preethi Anant.

Raza He seemed to like what we're doing the other night.

Jaz The man loves us.

Preethi You've got a nerve . . . it's bad enough you rock up at the *garba* without any notice. Didn't you get my text? I'm not dancing with you, Raza.

Raza Call me Raj.

Preethi It's not as if we're even going out.

Raza A month and a half . . . we're seeing each other.

Preethi Yeah, we're seeing each other, but it's not like Romeo and Juliet.

Raza I think it is.

Preethi Grow up

Raza It was nice to see you dressed up in your red and green . . .

Preethi Chanya Choli . . .

Raza You don't do that when we go Leicester Square . . . you put your jeans on like . . .

Preethi I wore my high heels last time.

Raza And I liked it.

Preethi So I did it.

Raza   I like it when your nostrils go like that . . .

Preethi   Don't push it.

Raza   And your eyebrows . . . the way you look away. Look at you.

Preethi   You're not getting round me. This competition is really important for my mum.

Raza   Got a Gujarati geek lined up?

Preethi   It's none of your business.

Raza   Jaz's got the hots for your mate. She gonna be here?

Preethi   Yeah. (*To* **Jaz**.) You better not get too fresh with her . . . Roopa doesn't know about you two.

Jaz   Chill. Thanks to you we're saucy, we're HPs . . . Hindu Punjabis.

Preethi   If anyone finds out you're SLIMS, literally hell is gonna come on earth.

Roopa *enters*.

Roopa   It's a bit of a surprise seeing you two.

Jaz   We're like wolves. We like to surprise. So you gonna do the Disco Dandia with me?

Roopa (*looking at* **Preethi**)   I dunno.

Preethi (*to* **Jaz**)   Her parents are really strict . . . I know you're Hindu, but they're even funny about Punjabis.

Raza   You girls wanna hook up this weekend?

Preethi   We're doing the competition Saturday.

Raza   Next weekend. We could go Park Royal . . . see a film. Chinese. You like Chinese?

Roopa   Don't mind.

Raza   There's an oriental buffet going on . . . prawn crackers, starters and shit like that . . . (*To girls.*) Have you seen *Bullet-Proof Monk*?

Roopa It's a bit violent, isn't it?

Jaz It's comic. Don't you like laughing?

Preethi *English Patient.* That's her favourite film.

Raza What?

Roopa It's a romance. In the desert.

Raza You want romance. You should come down my yard. I got *Kuch Kuch Hota Hai* on DVD. With extras.

Preethi *looks at* **Raza** *and he realises he's overstepped the limit by asking them to his place.*

Raza We could go bowling beforehand.

Roopa Do we look like the kind of girls who go bowling?

Hina *and* **Dinesh** *enter.*

Preethi All right, Hina? This is Jaz and Raj.

Jaz *and* **Raza**   Hi.

Hina Hi.

Preethi All right, *che* Dinesh?

Dinesh I'm fine. I've just installed the new application on your dad's Excel programme. It means he can pinpoint exactly what stock he's got in what outlet . . . serial number, model, quantity.

Preethi Great.

Dinesh It's totally revolutionary – it's like when Windows took over from MS DOS – everything's just a mouse-click away.

Preethi Fancy being my partner for Disco Dandia?

Hina He's already got a partner.

Anant *enters.*

Anant *Kemcho*, everyone? Hi, Preethi. Mummy, Daddy, okay? Dinesh, Jaz, Raj. Fantastic! I'm glad you took up my offer . . . great to have new blood in the class You guys blew my mind the other night. Raj, where did you learn to dance like that?

Raza On the street.

Jaz Nah man . . . it's from Ritek Roshan. He's taken his moves and added a bit of turbo.

Anant You guys are gonna put me out of business. Being able to do that with no training.

Jaz He's bad, innit? I'm not gay but I think he's bad.

Anant Yeah, the raw talent is there but needs a signature, Jaz. You can vouch, girls. How many times do you get picked out of a crowd and people say, 'The way you dance. You must be from the Anant Patel Academy.'

Hina We spread your fame, Anant.

Anant I'm a big fish in a small pond. You think this is everyone?

Hina Vinita rang to say she's gotta hand in her project. And Bharti's not feeling very well.

Anant And Seema?

Hina She'll be here.

Anant She's probably told Mummy she's coming here, but she's out with her boyfriend. Okay, let's start without her. Now you were all short-listed for Disco Dandia, you've got your partners. The Lohana Ladies season is open competition. You're all going to be challenging each other for the title of Diwali King and Queen, and hopefully you'll still be friends at the end of it.

Roopa Preethi's bound to win.

Hina Not necessarily.

Anant Roopa, that's not the attitude. You put your mind to something, you can do it. Positive thinking! Any of you could win, but let's make sure the winner is amongst us. We don't want those Patels from Tooting to walk away with the crowns. (*To* **Jaz** *and* **Raza**.) I'm a Patel myself, and I tell you, I was embarrassed. They go to that Beni Katania's South London Academy . . . She calls herself a choreographer but it's all thrusting bosoms and wriggling bums. Now, everybody, please go and get your sticks. We're gonna concentrate on putting the Disco into Dandia. (*Puts the music on.*)

Raza Chuck us a stick, Preethi.

Preethi *throws* **Raza** *a stick.*

Jaz (*to* **Roopa**) You up for it?

Roopa *nods.*

Anant Find a space in front of the mirror. We're going to start with the basic Dandia step. You hit your partner's stick for the first three counts, one, two three; do your own thing, four, five, six, seven, eight; and then hit again on the one; and then do freestyle for the next seven counts. Have you got that? Okay – let's have a go.

They dance.

Five, six, seven, eight.
   One, two, three and one.
   One, two, three and one.
   Okay, let's try it in pairs now. Find yourself a partner.
   One, two, three and one.
Change partners. Keep your sticks up. Six, seven, eight and one. Change again. One, two, three and one. Maintain eye-contact.
Okay. Let's form two lines facing each other – this time when you hit the stick on the one, you move to your left so you are facing a new dancing partner. Okay, you got that?

They move into the formation.

Left – that's it.

Okay – next time you do a turn when you move to your left.

And one.

Turn.

Okay, now show me what you can do, show me your best. Let's see who is the Sharukh Khan and Madhuri Dixit amongst you.

Okay, now clear the floor – we're going to work in pairs.

Raza *continues to dance while everyone else has stopped.*

Thank you, Raj. We'll start with Roopa and Jaz.

Roopa *and* **Jaz** *dance. After they finish,* **Anant** *calls* **Hina** *and* **Dinesh** *to the floor. They dance. They finish*

Anant Very nice, Dinesh – but don't forget to dance with your partner.

Anant *calls* **Preethi** *and* **Raza** *to the floor. They dance. They finish.*

Anant (*looking at* **Raza**) Fantastic. That was fantastic. I think we've just invented the Salsa Dandia.

Jaz You're fit, man. You should be setting the steps on those Bollywood films, man.

Anant They have their own choreographers. Very difficult to break in.

Jaz There's an Indian explosion, man. How come it's passed you by? These geezers, they come and film in Scotland . . . Tulip season in Amsterdam. You gotta find out.

Anant I should get you as my agent, Jaz.

Jaz Thirty-five per cent, mate.

Anant That was fantastic, guys! I'm gonna slot in another rehearsal tomorrow night. Seven o'clock. With some fine-tuning, we'll storm the Disco Dandia night. Okay, off you go now, go home – go home or wherever you have to go.

They all filter off. **Anant** *puts on the music and starts to dance as if working out a routine in his head.* **Prema** *enters.*

Anant *Prema bhen, Kemcho?* Your Preethi and her partner are good together.

Prema You think so? He's Punjabi, you know?

Anant He can dance.

Prema So she's in with a chance for Diwali Queen?

Anant Good as done.

Prema All my dedication has paid off. I had to drag her to your class when she was eight. And now the tables have turned. She can't miss it.

Anant It's nice to know that one has had some effect.

Pause.

Anant Can I do something for you?

Prema Anant, I . . . Last night there were a few complaints about the crisp flavours. The vegetarian lobby. Why not tell Shanti Bhen to keep ready-salted only?

Anant Of course . . .

Prema *Aao jo.*

Prema *starts to go and then stops.*

Anant Anything else?

Prema I know Mohan *bhai* says you're winding up your business . . .

Anant My father is speaking for me when nothing has been decided.

Prema I thought you were going to run the new underground outlet.

Anant If Bapu has his way, I will be a true Patel like him, running a newsagent.

Prema   So you might still have some room for a private student?

Anant   Preethi doesn't need extra coaching.

Prema   No, no, Anant. It's for me. Will you give me some steps for the dinner and dance? I'll of course give you your going rate.

Anant   No, no. It would be my pleasure.

Prema   It's just that Ketan is such a good dancer. I don't want to tread on his toes.

Anant   Yes, we fix it.

Prema   Tomorrow afternoon? My place. Will my new conservatory be suitable?

Anant   Perfect. After all, dinner and dance is about dancing effectively in a confined space.

Prema   So I'll see you tomorrow. *Aao jo.*

Anant   *Aao jo.*

Prema *leaves and* **Anant** *goes back to his dance.*

Scene Four

Same night. **Mohan** *and* **Anant***'s home. Three-bedroom suburban detached house in a cul-de-sac. Floral carpet, glass table and Hindu paraphernalia.*

Mohan   Lovely *kadhi*, Ba. At my age I should have my daughter-in-law serving my *rotlis*, not my mother.

Shanti   Be thankful there is food on your plate.

Mohan   To this day I don't know why Anant won't marry. He's married to his dancing.

Shanti   Leave it, Mohan.

Mohan   I'm thinking of you. Ba. If he had a wife you could go and live with Satish in Canada. They have Mexican maid who will look after you.

Shanti   I was prisoner when I went to visit your brother. Sat and watched video and got fat. Couldn't go anywhere without somebody driving me in a car.

Mohan   You should be pampered, Ba.

Shanti   I might as well be dead . . . I prefer to use my legs. Go to Ealing Road and get my fresh fruit and veg for your *rotlis* and *shaak*.

Mohan   And Anant can't even be bothered to show up for dinner on time.

Shanti   You should accept this is his passion. Navratri is the highlight of his year. This is where he can show off his talent. Of course he doesn't think about eating.

Mohan   Well, this is his last season.

Shanti   Why you are trying to turn him from choreographer to newsagent? If only you came once to see what his gift is, then you would change your mind.

Mohan   Navratri took my wife away from me. How can you ask me to go and celebrate?

Shanti   Varsha died because it was her time to go. You have been carrying this thing for too long now. Don't take it out on Anant.

The phone rings and **Mohan** *picks it up. We hear his side of the conversation.*

Mohan   Hello? . . . No. There is no dance academy here. This is a private residence . . . No, he is not here. This is Mohan Patel, his father. Who am I speaking with? . . . You want to leave message? You are producer of commercial? And you need choreographer of Dandia . . . well, my son is amateur . . . So what you want me to tell him? . . . You can't cast Gary Lineker as Krishna. He is the wrong

colour. Krishna is blue . . . Walker's Crisps. Good brand.
Sells well . . . I can tell you, my son will be too busy for
this. He's in business with me. We have a new outlet on the
Jubilee Line. If you need a shop to film in, that's another
story. (*Puts the phone down.*)

Shanti   It isn't for you to decide for the boy.

Mohan   I've given him his freedom. It's time for him to
get back on track. And I need all hands on deck. So don't
you go saying anything.

Anant *enters.*

Shanti   Food is ready. You must be tired after rehearsal.

Anant   I'm elated. Once in a while you see raw talent and
you know you can really shape it into something.

Shanti   You are really fired up. Who are you talking
about?

Anant   *Olo* Punjabi. Raj. He's dancing with Preethi. I know
I can give them advanced steps and they will be able to pull
it off.

Shanti   And the teacher? He needs to get some glory as
well.

Anant   I'm sure I'll make the cover of the *Lohana Ladies'
Bulletin.*

Mohan   How many years you've been teaching the
daughters of these society ladies? What have you got to show
for it?

Shanti   What are you talking about? A cupboard full of
cups and trophies he has won and who knows what is just
around the corner?

Mohan   Working in the new outlet is what's around the
corner.

Shanti   Aren't you going to tell him about his phone call?

Anant   What call?

Mohan   Nothing important.

Shanti   Not important? The man wanted Anant to give steps to Gary Lineker.

Anant   What was it about, Bapu?

Mohan   They are doing some advert. Yesterday it was bhangra, now it's *garba*. Where is that going to get you? I told them you wouldn't be interested.

Anant   You had no right to speak for me. Of course I am interested.

Mohan   You want to pursue some pipe dream while your father gets swallowed up by Tesco Metro and Sri Lankans who work round the clock. They can't even say 'please' and 'thank you', but still their tills are ringing. Half the time the customer wants their attention, they're on an international call arranging for one of their relatives to come over from Colombo as asylum cases and work for nothing.

Anant   Bapu, I know the shop is in trouble but I can't turn it round for you. I'm not a businessman. I keep telling you.

Mohan   And I keep telling you, you don't need a degree to be a businessman. Just you have to be by your father's side. That Navin from Tanzania. His son studied dentistry but still he made more money joining his father as newsagent. Now they are taking six holidays a year.

Anant   Good for them.

Mohan   That's all you can say. You invest in your children and you think you're going to get back with interest.

Shanti   Mohan!

Mohan   I've bought this underground kiosk so it can help to keep the other shop afloat. This is our last chance, otherwise he might as well go and tell those refugees they can have it on a plate.

Anant *leaves.*

Scene Five

Early evening. **Raza** *and* **Preethi** *run onto a bridge overlooking the Thames.*

Preethi So you booked our tickets for the London Eye?

Raza I'm not going on that . . . it hardly moves.

Preethi You're just like one of those White Hart Lane rude boys, aren't you? Everything fast. Fast food, fast cars . . . you don't want to take the time to take in the view?

Raza (*looking at her*) I've got all the time in the world to take in the view.

Preethi You want what you can't have.

Raza Doesn't stop me trying.

Preethi Look, we're doing the competition, then it's goodbye.

Raza You're keen when we're out, but you're quite happy to kiss me goodbye and hope one of those Gujarati frogs will turn into a prince.

Preethi Some of them are quite good-looking, actually.

Raza You still haven't told me which one's lined up for you.

Preethi We're not like you SLIMs, you know. I'm free to choose.

Raza So who have you chosen?

Preethi I haven't yet. But there's a hall full of boys every night. I'll take my pick when I'm ready.

Raza Having me dangling on your arm surely is gonna spoil your chances.

Preethi Not at all. Everyone knows you're just my dancing partner.

Raza I'm good, aren't I?

Preethi You can dance.

Raza We're good together.

Preethi You reckon yourself, don't you?

Raza Try that turn.

Preethi Not here.

Raza Why not?

Preethi You're crazy.

She does it reluctantly. They start to rehearse their routine together. The dance finishes.

Raza You wanna win, don't you?

Preethi Well my mum's the Chair. The spotlight's on me.

Raza How would you have won if I hadn't gate-crashed?

Preethi God – you love yourself, don't you.

Raza Gotta have belief, *Inshallah* . . .

Preethi You do realise if you're Diwali King, you're gonna be dressed up as Lord Ram on that float.

Raza The things I'd do for you.

Scene Six

Two days later. The Disco Dandia competition. A corner of the hall. A moment before the dancers are called.

Prema (*on tannoy*) It's the night you've been waiting for, guys and dolls – Disco Dandia! I can see the judges are going to have a tough time deciding who to eliminate and who to select as finalists for the grand finale on Saturday! Tonight we also have another spotlight on us as we have a special guest mingling anonymously looking for talent: choreographers, dancers, movers and shakers. Disco Dandia is taking centre stage. They want pretty girls and dashing boys and, looking around at this fashion parade, I can see that they're going to be spoilt for choice.

Anant (*to his students*)   You're all great . . . all the moves are really polished now. There won't be anybody better on the dance floor than you guys. Just believe in yourselves. Remember facial expression, smiling . . . it's just as important as fancy footwork . . . Presentation as well as execution. That's what the judges will be looking for. Okay, guys. You're all stars. Break a leg!

Preethi *and* **Raza, Roopa** *and* **Jaz, Hina** *and* **Dinesh** *take their positions on the dance floor.*

Jaz   So you told your parents you're dancing with a Hindu Punjabi?

Roopa   Didn't need to.

Jaz   But aren't they watching us?

Roopa   No, they'd rather stay home and watch *EastEnders*. Suits me . . . As long as I check in on my moby every twenty minutes they're cool. Preethi and Raj look like they've been putting in some extra rehearsal.

Jaz   Yeah.

Roopa   That's Preethi all over. She'd say she hadn't revised for her Maths, then she'd get a straight A.

Jaz   Don't worry. I beat Raj at everything.

Hina (*to Dinesh*)   I'm gonna marry you.

Dinesh   My dad's got Preethi in mind for me.

Hina   I know your dad's her dad's accountant, but she's a Louis and you and I are Shahs, Dinesh.

Dinesh   So what?

Hina   What they call *halva*, we call *halvo*. If you don't get a move on, I'm registering for that Shah speed dating. I'm not going to be available next year.

Sonya   I heard those Louis tarts talking about that talent scout in the toilets. They shut up the minute I came out of the loo. You know they're making an ad. The old lady off the Kumars marries Gary Lineker. Just think, I could be sharing the small screen with Meera Syal.

Shrenek   The close-up will be on you, babe.

Sonya   Your shimmy's gonna wipe the floor. When I saw that at Wandsworth Town Hall. That's when I decided . . . this is the man I'm gonna dance with.

Shrenek   What about the rest?

Sonya   Don't go on about that. I told you. I'm focused on the future.

Preethi and **Raza** are dancing and he looks at her intimately.

Preethi   Everyone's looking at us.

Raza   Yeah, 'cos we're the best.

Preethi   Nah, it's 'cos they all think I've snuck my Hindu Punjabi boyfriend in. God, if they knew the truth.

The dance speeds up. **Raza** and **Jaz** are being more exuberant. **Jaz** hits **Shrenek**'s stick too hard.

Shrenek (to **Jaz**)   What's with the stick flex, mate?

Jaz   What you on about?

Shrenek   You bang my stick so hard, you nearly bang it out of my hand.

Dance ends.

Prema (on tannoy)   Thank you, boys and girls. That was fantastic. Now could we please clear the floor for Contestants 36 to 40.

Scene Seven

Car park. Just outside. A little while later. **Roopa** *and* **Jaz** *are kissing.*

Jaz   You were rough on the dance floor. We're bound to be chosen.

Roopa   I can't believe you've never done Dandia.

Jaz   It's in my blood. I've got a great place to rehearse for the finale.

Roopa   Where?

Jaz   Raj's flat in Kew Gardens. Got a wicked Playstation, sauna, jacuzzi . . . fridge . . . kitchen kitted out.

Preethi, **Raza**, **Hina** *and* **Dinesh** *enter.*

Raza   Is that talent scout business for real?

Preethi   Yeah, my mum got a phone call about it. The Louis ladies are getting all excited.

Hina   It's not just the Lohanas he rang, you know. My mum said they're ringing round all the Navratri committees.

Dinesh   Might be a hoax. Guy rings up says he's a talent scout. All the 'stay at home' *gujus* come out thinking they might become stars . . . halls are bursting to the seams. Bombs go off simultaneously. Bingo! What better way of getting rid of the Gujarati community in one go?

Roopa   Whatever, Dinesh. Adds to the excitement.

Sonya *and* **Shrenek** *enter.*

Shrenek   I've been looking for you. What do you think you were doing in there?

Jaz   Dunno what you talking about, big boy.

Shrenek   Hit my stick too hard.

Jaz   You got a over-active imagination.

Shrenek   You're trying to distract me and ruin my chances.

Jaz   You think you're competition?

Sonya   What you talking about? We're the only movers here. You're just intimidated by our steps.

Shrenek   Doesn't have to come down to violence.

Jaz   You pussy. It's Dandia. You can't be timid about hitting the stick.

Sonya   Hitting the stick like you did implies a challenge. I saw it.

Jaz   Hey, lady. I'm talking to your man.

Raza   Come on, Jaz. Leave it out.

Shrenek   I saw the look you gave me.

Jaz   I'm dancing. I'm concentrating. What look did I give you?

Shrenek   That look there. You looking at me funny? What are you looking at me like that for?

Jaz   You must be gay. The man must be gay.

Sonya   Takes one to know one.

Jaz   Get out of my face.

Raza   Jaz. It's not worth it.

Shrenek   You bang my stick like that again, I'll bang you back.

Jaz   Just try it.

Shrenek   What are you gonna do? Bring your bad boys from Punjab?

Jaz   We'll bring our whole crew down.

Shrenek   I'm not scared of you, gay boy.

Jaz *strikes* **Shrenek**, *and* **Raza** *tries to intervene.*

Preethi Jaz! Raza!

Sonya Raza . . . This is revelation time. I thought it was Raj . . .

Shrenek That says it all. Mosis coming in on Hindu territory.

Sonya Who brought them in?

Preethi They're my friends.

Roopa He's a Muslim, you *kutti*, why didn't you tell me?

Jaz I'm the same guy.

Roopa We don't go there, yeah . . . I don't go there. (*To* **Preethi** *as she's leaving.*) People don't do that to their worst enemies.

Shrenek Any girl that goes with a Muslim needs her head looking at. Didn't you hear about the rape last Navratri? That was a Muslim. You're after our girls . . . keep your sisters locked up at home.

Raza *goes for* **Shrenek** *and they fight, with the others trying to stop them.* **Dinesh** *intervenes to try and stop them.*

Hina (*to* **Dinesh**) Don't you get involved. It's not us who brought them in.

Prema *and* **Anant** *come on.*

Prema Preethi! What is going on?

Anant Stop it, boys.

The fight breaks up.

Prema When I heard there was a scuffle out here, the last person I expected to be involved was you.

Sonya It was them that started it, not us.

Prema Fighting leads to immediate disqualification.

Sonya You should disqualify them. They come in here under false pretences . . . they're looking for trouble. They're not dancers, they're Muslims.

Prema Darling, is this true?

Preethi Yes, Mum.

Prema And you knew?

Preethi Yes.

Prema So you were all in on this deceit?

Hina Prema aunty, Dinesh and I knew nothing about this.

Prema After all the freedom I've given you. Kick-boxing lessons . . . navel-piercing . . . anything you've asked for. Your generation thinks us to be idiots. Why you didn't just come and tell me you want to bring some friends from college or wherever? When have we ever stopped people coming? . . . We allow black people, English . . . as long as they come with Gujarati friends and behave appropriately.

Raza It's not Preethi's fault we gate-crashed.

Prema I don't know what your parents expect from you, Raj . . .

Raza Raza.

Prema . . . but I expect better from my daughter.

Sonya Are you going to disqualify them?

Raza You don't need to. Come on, Jaz.

Anant You shouldn't have lied, guys. It's a shame.

Jaz *and* **Raza** *leave.*

Preethi Mum . . .

Prema I don't wish to hang out our linen in the car park. Get your things and let's go.

Hina So you still gonna dance, Preethi?

They all leave apart from **Anant***, who sits down and takes out the card that the scout has given him.*

Mohan Ready, son? Kiosk all packed up.

Anant   Nearly. Ba is finishing up.

Mohan   You'll have to be more cheerful when you're dealing with customers. Talk to them about their highs and lows instead of showing yours.

Anant   There was a fight.

Mohan   I thought Prema forked out a fortune for Nigerian security. Who was involved?

Anant   My students.

Mohan   Youngsters are more interested in fighting and sex than your dancing. Good you're coming to work with me. You won't have to bother with the likes of them.

Anant   Bapu, I don't see myself as a newsagent.

Mohan   So how do you see yourself? A tortured artist?

Anant   Dance is all I know.

Mohan   Dance doesn't pay the bills.

Anant   It could. That man who rang up at home asking for me. Julian. Well, he found me even though you tried to stop him. I've got talent. He's coming to the finale.

Mohan   Stop this 'dance, dance, talent, talent' . . . what is this talent? Stopping you living your life. You start work with me. From six a.m., taking newspaper delivery to late at night. You won't have time to think about your talent.

Anant   You would love that for me? You've never even seen any of my work.

Mohan   I've seen enough what dance does to people. It takes possession of you like it took possession of your mother. She would dance till she thought the goddess came to her. People would worship her, but who was there to help her when the dance took her?

Anant   Bapu, she was an epileptic. It could have happened at any time.

Mohan   No, it happened in this season of Navratri, and now you are trying to kill me with your dance.

Anant   All right. Enough. In any case I've lost my best student, so what is there for Julian to see at the finale? Fine. Next week. Six a.m. I'll be there. Happy now?

Scene Eight

The community hall, which has been decorated for the dinner and dance. A ship in the sixties, on its journey from Dar es Salaam to Bombay. **Popatlal** *and* **Pushpa**, *in Prema's black and white theme, are standing on what looks like the deck of a ship eating* chana bateta *and with tall drinks in their hands.* **Shanti** *is serving food in this scene.*

Pushpa   It is Prema's daughter that brings in the Muslims and it is my daughter that is suffering! Dinesh and Hina entered as a couple. Now Hina is in her bedroom crying with no partner, and Dinesh has been ordered by his papa to dance with Preethi . . . as if that's going to save her reputation!

Popatlal   Prema is taking advantage of her role as Chair. Changing the rules to suit.

Pushpa   Hina and Dinesh have been virtually engaged since they were eight . . . everyone knows. (*To* **Shanti**.) This coconut in the *chana bateta* isn't fresh.

Shanti   From the packet . . . tastes the same.

Pushpa   And the Mogo chips are frozen. It's all very well having East African theme, but Prema should have made sure she got the food right.

Bharat *enters.*

Pushpa (*to* **Popatlal**)   Think of your daughter. Go and talk to Bharat.

Popatlal   This incident in the car park has upset the apple cart.

Bharat   A couple of outsiders come in . . . they've got green eyes. Of course our girls are going to swoon over them. Prema nipped it in the bud.

Pushpa   They didn't just come in. They were invited. They were introduced to us as Preethi's 'friends'.

Bharat   The way our community likes to make a mountain out of a molehill.

Pushpa   Going behind parents' backs is something Hina would never do. And she certainly wouldn't steal someone else's partner.

Bharat   Pushpa *bhen*, who holds the strings to the hearts of youngsters? Until they are engaged, they are free to change their minds. Dinesh and Preethi want to dance with each other.

Pushpa   Our daughter is not going to be anybody's 'back-up'.

Prema *enters.*

Bharat   Prema, *bhen*. You have transported us back to the port of Dar es Salaam. You can almost smell the sea breeze.

Prema   So you like the idea of the ship? Cocktails on deck before departure, virgin of course, and then we sail on to Bombay via the Seychelles, and all in one evening . . . Pushpa *bhen*, you look like Cinderella at the ball.

Pushpa   Blouse is a bit tight, *he ne*? I'll have to go to the gym.

Popatlal   Half an hour on the treadmill, you come back and raid the fridge.

Pushpa   And where is your Prince Charming, Prema?

Popatlal   More than fashionably late.

Prema   He'll be here. People are starting to dance. Please join them. Bharat *bhai*, there's plenty of mature single ladies waiting to have their card filled.

Pushpa (*under her breath to* **Popatlal**)   Most of them are at an age when they should be singing devotional songs at home.

They go onto the dance floor and start dancing. **Prema** *exits, obviously anxious that* **Ketan** *isn't there.* **Preethi** *and* **Dinesh** *enter and stand leaning on the ship's railings.*

Dinesh   Drowning is one of easiest ways, I suppose, to top yourself . . . otherwise it's not that easy.

Preethi   I'm not contemplating suicide, Dinesh.

Dinesh   No, no, it's just interesting . . . you know, there's this site where you can find out the most effective ways: what's a lethal dose . . . how to tie the knot . . . prime locations – that bridge over Archway Road, the cliff at Beachy Head . . .

Preethi   You don't want to dance with me at the finale, do you?

Dinesh   No, no, it's fine.

Preethi   I've got a bit of a 'rep' now. If you want to dance with Hina, it's okay with me.

Dinesh   Where d'you meet that Raza guy, anyway?

Preethi   Outside the sweet shop.

Dinesh   He didn't seem like one of those prayer-mat types.

Preethi   Raza is one of the sweetest fellas you could ever meet. It just happens he's a Muslim.

Dinesh   At the end of the day you gotta stick within.

Preethi   Why? Why? I'm sick of this, you know . . . you're a Lohanna, or Shah, Patel . . . whatever . . . so-and-so's daughter from such-and-such village, and after marriage you become so-and-so's wife from his village. Everyone's got roots. What's so special about Gujaratis?

Dinesh   Our parents do so much for us. How do you pay them back?

Preethi   So that's what you're doing with me?

The focus shifts to the dance, which is now in full swing. **Prema** *and* **Anant** *have now joined as a couple.* **Preethi** *and* **Dinesh** *exit.*

Prema   Thanks for partnering me.

Anant   I can see you've been practising.

Prema   Yes, but what for?

Anant   I'm sure Ketan *bhai* will be here soon.

Prema   It's nine o'clock already. If he was coming, he would have been here by now, Anant.

Anant   Maybe he has got delayed in his business.

Prema   Maybe he just doesn't care.

Anant   Prema *bhen* . . .

Prema   Having to deal with people's comments about Preethi is bad enough. And now this? Ketan knows how much I have put into this evening, but he is not interested. Single-handedly I have organised each detail, even though I have got a sub-committee. The fruit display . . . I told Sita, use your initiative. The float ran out, so she buys three apples. How can you make an impact with three apples? You saw everyone, how they were looking at me. Pushpa is thoroughly enjoying my humiliation on the dance floor, seeing me without my husband on a night I'm hosting while hers is stuck to her like a Siamese twin.

Anant   Prema *bhen*, nobody is looking at you.

Prema   Believe me, I know them. Women like her, false nails and imitation jewellery . . . they would enjoy nothing better than to see my downfall. I am the Chair of Lohana Ladies. My functions are talked about and copied. In a million years Pushpa couldn't come up with my concepts. She is just watching, watching to see me put a foot wrong so she can step into the breach and have her victory.

Anant Why you are worrying about other people?

Prema You're right, Anant. I spend my life trying to please other people. I try to make everything just right, but no matter how much effort I put I can't seem to fix what's broken.

Anant It's a perfect evening, Prema *bhen*. Everyone appreciates what you do.

Prema Everyone except the person you want to appreciate you. To him I am invisible.

Silence.

Prema I'm sorry. I shouldn't burden you with my problems. I'm sure you have plenty of your own.

Anant None that a dose of hard labour at the shop won't fix.

Prema You're going to join Mohan *bhai* in the shop? It's a shame.

Anant I'm sure nobody will miss their Gujarati ballet class in Bounds Green.

Prema But that Julian was very impressed with you. He's coming at the finale just to see your work.

Anant If he could have seen Raj . . . Raza and Preethi dance.

Prema My hands are tied, Anant.

Anant Of course. Shall we dance to 'Malaika'? It would be a shame not to show off what you've learnt.

The next dance starts to the classic Swahili hit and they go back onto the floor.

Prema Thank you, Anant.

Scene Nine

Later that night. **Prema**'s *conservatory.* **Prema** *and* **Preethi** *are having a glass of wine.*

Preethi   Are you waiting up for Dad?

Prema   I'm just finishing my wine.

Preethi   It was a great evening. Did they really have dinner and dances on those ships?

Prema   Of course, but only in first class. The people dancing were the Europeans.

Preethi   You were good. I didn't know you could dance like that.

Prema   I can't. It was down to Anant.

Preethi   Secret lessons – whatever next?

Prema   At least my secrets are harmless.

Preethi   I'm sorry, Mum.

Prema   We've never restricted you in any way.

Preethi   I know, Mum. But sometimes you meet someone and they don't have a label stuck to their head.

Prema   But now you've got a label stuck to yours.

Ketan *enters.*

Preethi   Hi, Dad.

Ketan   Did you get my message?

Prema   The one you left at ten o'clock, just as dinner was being served?

Ketan   Sorry, darling, I fully intended to be there . . . You know these Arabs. They like to eat late. By the time I could get round to ringing you, it was already ten.

Prema   You had a previous engagement . . . with me.

Ketan So how did it go?

Prema Oh, it was fantastic . . . Everybody had a great time gabbing about our daughter and her reputation, and seeing me partnered by the 'camp choreographer' was the icing on the cake.

Preethi Mum, Dad said he was sorry.

Prema Yes, both of you have said sorry and sorry makes it all right, *ne*? Mummy is always here to pick up the pieces. Prema will put on her lipstick and smile at everyone. 'No, no . . . not my daughter. My daughter doesn't abuse her freedom . . . ' 'Definitely not my husband . . . he is working hard . . . family man . . . always working late making sure his princess is well provided for.' (*To* **Ketan**.) I make it so easy for you . . . When do I ask you for anything?

Ketan I know, darling. I know you do a lot for us, but I'm also working so you can have things you want . . . car, conservatory.

Prema Is that all you think I need?

Ketan I know I've neglected you, but I'll make it up to you. I had my travel agent book the resort in Dubai for our silver wedding anniversary. Seven-star treatment.

Prema Meanwhile I have to be satisfied with zero-star treatment?

Ketan You have everything. I'm sure many women would love to be in your shoes.

Prema Oh, I know . . . don't think I don't know you already have someone in my shoes.

Preethi Mum!

Prema Ask him! Ask him where he was when he knew how important it was for me to have him at the dinner and dance . . .

Ketan I've already told you. You can't offend Arabs.

Prema   Ask him why his secretary chooses my birthday presents when he has time to choose gifts for his . . . mistress.

Ketan   I haven't got the energy for this. I've got a breakfast meeting in the morning.

Ketan *leaves.*

Preethi   Is it true, Mummy?

Prema   What do you think?

Preethi   I can't believe Dad would do that.

Prema   Why? Because your daddy is perfect? Must be Mummy imagining things . . . All I asked is for him to be at my side for one night, and he couldn't even do that . . .

Preethi   Oh, poor Mum.

Her phone signals a text message.

Prema   Who is sending you messages at this time?

Prema *takes* **Preethi**'s *phone and* **Raza**'s *name comes up.*

Prema   Like father, like daughter. Keeping secrets from me.

Preethi   I told Raza not to phone me.

Prema   And you expect me to believe that?

Preethi   Give me my phone.

Prema (*giving her back her phone*)   I've done my best with you . . . You're lucky that Bharat Shah wants to suck up to your daddy and is willing to overlook the gossip . . . Apart from Dinesh, there is no Gujarati boy in London for you.

Preethi *looks at her text message.*

Preethi   Mum, something's happened to Mohan uncle. Raza's outside . . . he needs to speak to you.

Prema   Why doesn't he ring the bell like a man?

Preethi *goes to let* **Raza** *in.*

Raza   I'm sorry to disturb you at this time.

Prema   Come in.

Preethi   What's happened?

Raza   Jaz and I were waiting for the tube . . . we went into a kiosk to buy some chewing gum. Two guys came running out as soon as they saw us. . . . They'd attacked this geezer in the shop . . . turned out he was Anant's dad.

Prema   Is he all right?

Raza   He's more shaken than hurt but they want to keep him overnight at the hospital. Anant's with him.

Prema   Poor Mohan *bhai.*

Raza   Anant wanted me to give you the float and keys for tomorrow night. He and Shanti won't be able to open the stall.

Prema   Of course. It must have been a terrible shock for her. Where is she?

Raza   She's in the van. Anant asked me to drop her home.

Prema   I'll go and see her.

Raza   She's fast asleep. Call her tomorrow. I've unloaded the crisps and drinks. Where do you want them?

Prema   In the garage.

Raza   I wanted to say sorry for any trouble I caused.

Prema   Anant is very disappointed you won't be in the finale.

Raza   So am I.

Prema   You should have thought twice before deceiving people.

Preethi   It was me who introduced him as Raj.

Raza   Preethi, I came in myself. I wanted to see your life.

Prema   Well, curiosity killed the cat. Preethi will show you the garage.

Preethi and **Raza** *leave.* **Prema** *is left alone. She exits.*

Scene Ten

A few seconds later. **Preethi** *and* **Raza** *come on with crisp boxes that they put in the garage.*

Raza   I missed you.

Preethi *doesn't say anything.*

Raza   So you haven't missed me, then?

Preethi   What would be the point?

Raza   What's wrong?

Preethi   What's right? (*Noticing a scratch on* **Raza***'s face.*) What's that?

Raza   Just a scratch.

Preethi   Been in a fight?

Raza   Those geezers. Jaz and I had to pull them off Anant's dad.

Preethi   Why didn't you tell my mum the full story?

Raza   She's still got the hump with me. I didn't want to be playing the hero.

Preethi   D'ya blame her?

Preethi   Just 'cos Gandhi was a Gujarati doesn't mean we can't get angry.

Raza   I didn't want it to happen like this.

Preethi   When you rocked up at the *garba* you changed the rules. What did you expect would happen?

Raza When I checked you outside the sweetshop, I thought, I wanna get to know this woman . . . really get to know her.

Preethi So you chatted me up . . . talked the talk, made the right moves.

Raza It's not just talk you know . . . we can make it real.

Preethi What's real? Everything you think is real turns out to be pretend.

Raza What are you talking about?

Preethi Nothing.

Raza I love you

Preethi Every Guju girl's got a friend who's been seeing a SLIM for years, only to find that the bloke goes back to Pakistan when it comes to marriage.

Raza And you think I'm going to do that?

Preethi I dunno . . . your parents are out there . . . What are they gonna say about me? It can't be me against the world.

Raza Let me talk to your parents.

Preethi It's the biggest time of the year for my mum, and it all had to happen now.

Raza Doesn't have to be the end of us.

Preethi Look, we went out, few drinks, had a laugh but it's not very funny now. You're a great guy, Raza, but . . .

Raza No buts . . . (*Holding her closer and starting to dance.*) I'm not letting go of you . . . we'll take it a bit slower.

Preethi There ain't nothing to take slower. (**Preethi** *dances, her actions contradicting her words.*) It was nothing in the first place.

They say goodbye, through dancing the duet that they should have danced at the finale. At a moment in the dance, **Shanti** *comes on and observes unseen.* **Preethi** *exits.*

Shanti   I was getting cold waiting in the van, I thought Prema had exiled you to the forest.

Raza   Well, she wants me as far away from her daughter as possible.

Shanti   People see it as Bhagwan versus Allah and not about Preethi and Raza.

Raza   You should have told me the score on that first night that Jaz and me gate-crashed.

Shanti   And you would have listened?

Raza *doesn't answer.*

Shanti   Wisdom only comes from living your own life, not walking down the path that others have laid.

Raza   Look, Preethi and I have said goodbye.

Shanti   So you're going to let her dance with Dinesh Shah?

Raza   You're kidding? She didn't say.

Shanti   Bharat Shah is taking advantage of the scandal. He has always had designs on Preethi for his Dinesh.

Raza   That's her lookout now.

Shanti   You're young . . . you have to fight for what you want in this world.

Raza   Well, Preethi comes from a different world and they won't let me in . . . Look, can I ask you a favour?

Shanti   The way you came to my son's aid, you can ask for anything from me.

Raza   Will you call me on Saturday? When Preethi's crowned Diwali Queen?

Shanti   You're so certain it will be her.

Raza   Yeah. Even with Dinesh as her partner.

Shanti   Yes, she's like the garbo pot. She has an inner light.

Raza I'll give you my number. You will call?

Shanti Of course. Son and grandson have bought me a mobile. Even though I'm never out of their sight for long.

Raza Come on.

Scene Eleven

Gymnasium. Evening. The grand finale. As in Scene One, characters are sitting on the grandstand waiting before they go onto the floor. **Roopa, Dinesh** *and* **Preethi, Sonya** *and* **Shrenek, Bharat, Ketan, Popatlal** *and* **Pushpa.** *We see* **Prema** *making an announcement on the tannoy.*

Prema We are nearly at the culmination of our season. Tension among the finalists here at the grand finale is thicker than the fog and the traffic on the North Circular tonight. So far our eminent guests, dignitaries and of course our esteemed judges, the Mayor and Mayoress, have been treated to an evening of innovation and interpretation. Dandia has never been more dazzling. We are almost there. Shahs, Patels and Lohanas are evenly matched. But who knows? The final four couples could tip the balance! Watch this space! As you youngsters would say. I'll soon be announcing the final couples.

Preethi I'm so nervous. Hope I don't muck up the body-popping bit.

Dinesh Just let me lead.

Preethi The crowd clapometer is certainly not going to be with us.

Dinesh It's about how well we dance, not how popular we are.

Preethi Well, I'd lose in the popularity stakes. The way that Sonya looked at me in the loos, you'd think I had SARS. (*Indicating* **Roopa.**) And there's another one who's blanking me out. Roops and I go back years.

Roopa *exits.*

Dinesh   Yeah, Hina and I used to do 'speak and spell' together. Look at encyclopedias . . . planets, capital cities, that sort of thing.

Preethi   Where is Hina? Isn't she dancing?

Dinesh   Don't know. She's blocked my address on her e-mail. My messsages keep bouncing back to me.

Preethi   It's all my fault, isn't it? What a mess.

Dinesh   Dad's set his heart on us winning.

Preethi   And we can't disappoint our parents, can we?

Our focus goes to **Pushpa** *and* **Popatlal**.

Pushpa   That Bharat has really got Ketan Datani in his pocket now. He's going around with his Colgate smile. You wait and see. The wedding invitations are probably at the printers already.

Popatlal   Bharat is Ketan's spin doctor, *neh*? Wiping out the scandal so the Datanis can come out smiling.

Pushpa   *Han*, the Lohanas get what they want and they don't care how and now Dinesh is lost to us.

Popatlal   Poor Hina. She's missed most of the competition. She should have come with us.

Pushpa   She'll be here. She's ironing her hair and plucking her eyebrows to look anonymous. I said to her, forget Dinesh, still might meet a match. She's a year younger than Preethi Datani and no black marks on her character . . . She's got another season. Let's go wait outside for her. Not nice to walk in alone.

We focus on **Prema**, **Ketan** *and* **Bharat**.

Bharat (*looking at* **Dinesh** *and* **Preethi**)   Our children look so good together.

Ketan   My princess lights up any room she walks into.

Bharat   The home she enters will be blessed.

Ketan   That is for sure.

Bharat   And these days . . . caste . . . what does it matter?
Shah, Lohanna . . . I say to Dinesh . . . Gujarati girl will
do. Of course, you and I know each other very well . . .
I don't need to investigate what village you are from.

Ketan   You give children choice . . . all the sweets are
there . . . I know Preethi will pick the right one.

Bharat   *Han.* We parents have done our bit.

Bharat *shakes* **Ketan**'*s hand and goes.*

Prema   Why are you letting Bharat think that we're going
to allow Preethi to marry Dinesh?

Ketan   That is my intention.

Prema   What? Without discussing it with Preethi or me?

Ketan   When she abused her freedom, she sealed her fate.

Prema   Why don't you look at some Lohana boys overseas
through the golf club?

Ketan   The golf club? They're all talking about her. I can't
set foot in there.

Prema   Isn't she allowed one mistake in life?

Ketan   She could have chosen who she wants, but she
knew the boundaries and she crossed over them.

Prema   And you think she's going to say yes to your
plans?

Ketan   How else are we going to save face?

Prema   Everything we do in our lives is just to save face,
isn't it?

Ketan   I'm going to greet my clients. You haven't acknow-
ledged my firm yet. We have sponsored the whole evening.

Ketan *and* **Prema** *exit. Our focus shifts to* **Sonya** *and* **Shrenek**.

Sonya   I've already introduced myself to the Mayor and Mayoress.

Shrenek   Bit eager! You should have waited till we'd danced.

Sonya   Nah! You gotta be one step ahead. It's good for the judges to put a face to the winners.

Shrenek   And what a face . . . hair really works.

Sonya   Took me five hours. Heated rollers, serum on each individual strand . . . can't wait to get a personal stylist. When we win and get that commercial, we'll be able to get our glossies done for free, invitations to premières, paparazzi following us around.

Shrenek   Sonya and Shrenek will be in a different league.

Prema (*on the tannoy*)   I just want to take a moment to remind everyone, especially the dancers who are chewing their nails backstage, everyone's a winner tonight! You've all done tremendously well to get to this stage, so all of you will walk away with at least a memento. Prizes and indeed today's entire event is sponsored by leading electronics firm Datani Sparks! The MD Mr Ketan Datani's mission is to add a sparkle to everyday lives! And judging by the prizes he will certainly succeed in that. Top prizes range from electronic calculators to electric toothbrushes to keep you smiling! It's back to the contest in just a moment.

Mohan *enters.*

Shanti   What are you doing here, son?

Mohan   I haven't missed Anant's students, have I? The programme said that they were on towards the end?

Shanti   Since when have you taken an interest in this?

Mohan   At least I'm here.

Shanti   Well, it's too little too late. What is Anant going to do with your interest now? You have already tethered him to your shop.

Mohan   Ba, stepping foot into a Navratri is big step for me.

Anant *enters.*

Anant What are you doing here, Bapu?

Mohan Son, I wanted to see what you do before it's too late.

Anant Why are you talking like that? You have plenty of time ahead of you.

Mohan Who knows with life? Look what happened to me, even with twenty-four-hour CCTV cameras. Tomorrow there might be a terrorist on the underground.

Anant Well, you're not going back there again. It's my responsibility to see how both outlets are manned.

Shanti Have you talked to that Julian at least?

Anant What's the point?

Mohan Punjabis have been fashionable for long enough.

Shanti He's interested in you. Go and explain to him why Raza isn't dancing. He'll understand.

Anant There's no need.

Mohan Raza. Who is he?

Shanti *Olo chokra* . . . Raza . . . the same one who saved you from those rough boys.

Mohan What a brave boy! Putting his life at risk for me. I didn't know he was Anant's student.

Shanti Not just student . . . his prize student for the competition.

Mohan A Muslim? His prize student? How did that happen?

Anant It's a long story.

Shanti Those Patels from Tooting are buttering up that TV man. If you don't show him that you're keen, their teacher Beni Katania is going to get the choreography job.

Anant   Let her have her five minutes of fame.

Anant *leaves.*

Shanti   If only Raza was dancing, Anant would have his showcase.

Mohan   I wanted to offer him and his friend a reward.

Shanti   I have his number on my mobile.

Mohan *and* **Shanti** *leave.*

Prema (*on tannoy*)   Here we are! The final contestants of the grand finale. It gives me great pleasure to invite Miss Roopa Kotecha and Mr Kalpesh Tanna to the floor.

Roopa *and* **Kalpesh** *dance.*

Prema   And now, hot contenders for the title, Sonya and Shrenek Patel, from Beni Katania's South London Dance Academy.

Sonya *and* **Shrenek** *are cheered on and they dance.*

Prema   And finally Miss Preethi Datani and Mr Dinesh Shah.

Preethi *and* **Dinesh** *are cheered onto the floor. They take their positions but, before they start,* **Raza** *enters and stops everyone in their tracks.*

Raza   Mrs Datani, I would like your permission to dance with Preethi.

Sonya   But he's been disqualified.

Raza   Mrs Datani, you have disqualified me from the dance competition, but don't disqualify me from competing for Preethi's heart. I know I shouldn't have come here but someone told me that I should fight for what I want in life and my life is nothing without your daughter. I don't want to take her away from all this. I want to be a part of it.

Dinesh *steps aside for* **Raza**.

Bharat What do you think you're doing, son? Everything I've done is to get you to this place. You're throwing away your passport to happiness.

Dinesh No, Dad. Hina is my partner. I should never have let her go. (*To* **Prema**.) Mrs Datani, if Hina is here, I would like to dance with Hina Shah.

Hina *enters, clearly showing her delight.*

Dinesh Will you please announce us?

Prema Ladies and gentlemen, there has been a slight change in the line-up for this evening. We will now have Miss Hina Shah and Mr Dinesh Shah, followed by Miss Preethi Datani and Mr Raza . . .?

Raza Khan.

Sonya Changing rules when they feel like it!

Shrenek Don't worry, babes. He can't touch us.

Ketan Are you out of your mind? Stop this madness.

Prema Why? So Preethi can keep up the pretence for your sake?

Ketan Why are you humiliating me? In front of clients? Community?

Prema You didn't mind humiliating me in front of the same community. Everyone knows about you. They don't say, but they talk behind your back. I have kept quiet for too long, painting a perfect picture of our life which was false, but I won't have my daughter living a lie.

Ketan You think Preethi is going to thank you when he has left her for a virgin in purdah and she is left with no prospects?

Prema Preethi and I can live with the consequences of our actions. Can you live with the consequences of yours?

Ketan *leaves.*

Prema   Music, please.

Music comes on. **Hina** *and* **Dinesh** *dance.*

Prema   And now for the final couple of the season, Miss Preethi Datani and Mr Raza Khan.

Raza *and* **Preethi** *dance. The crowd is uncertain how to react.*

Prema   I'm sure the judges would like to take a couple of moments to deliberate. I will be back with the results soon.

Focus shifts to **Bharat** *and* **Popatlal**.

Popatlal   You see, Bharat *bhai*, they use you and spit you out when it suits them.

Bharat   *Han*, you were right, *bhai*. I should have stuck with the Shahs, instead of trying to build bridges. As Ketan's accountant, I got to know his ins and outs, but I wasn't expecting this from the daughter.

Popatlal   Well, you have our guarantee that we have no skeletons in our cupboard.

Bharat   Dinesh is very lucky that you are willing to forgive and forget.

Popatlal   We have to look forward, *he ne*? No point to dwell backwards.

Bharat   *Han*. Let's end the season with an official announcement of the engagement. With my connections, we can get this hall for the wedding if you want.

Popatlal   Even with both families and friends this hall is too big, *he ne*? But for next year's Navratri?

Bharat   Goes without saying. It's time for the Shahs to take control of our cultural heritage.

Popatlal   Yes. Integration is all very well but it has its place. This sort of dilution leads to pollution. Preethi and her partner danced well. A Muslim could be waving from the number one float and switching on the Diwali lights.

Bharat   God forbid, and I'm sure His Worshipful would agree with us. Normally I wouldn't use my influence with him, but desperate circumstances call for desperate measures.

He exits to talk to the Mayor and Mayoress.

Prema   Now for the moment we've all been waiting for. The judges have deliberated and I have the envelope here with the results. I will announce them in reverse order. (*She opens the envelope and reads.*) In third place, Miss Hema Patel and Mr Ritesh Shah. In second place we have Sonya and Shrenek Patel . . .

Sonya *shrieks in disbelief.*

Sonya   This is a stitch-up. Bet it's that SLIM and his *slag.*

Shrenek   Next time, eh, babe?

Sonya   What next time? I've been talking to Julian. He said you were holding me back. I'm going *solo.*

Shrenek   Babe?

Sonya Oh, piss off! (*Storms off.*)

Prema   And finally. The judges would like to crown Miss Hina Shah and Mr Dinesh Shah as the Diwali Queen and Diwali King. Hina and Dinesh will head the Diwali parade and take home with them his-and-her foot-massage machines. Please come forward.

Hina *gushingly drags* **Dinesh** *forward.* **Shanti** *crowns* **Hina** *and* **Dinesh**.

Dinesh   I know how much it means to my dad to see me wearing this, and I just want you to know, Dad, that you brought me up to work hard, be better than anyone else and to get by on merit. That is what winning this competition was about for me, not about being a Shah, Patel or Lohana. Everyone here knows who the real winners are. I'm sorry I can't accept this crown.

He takes off his crown and hands it back. **Hina** *follows his example.*

Prema   Bravo! How gracefully this young man has spoken. You're a credit to your parents. When I proposed this intercaste competition, I had no idea just how much of a challenge I was going to face. You young people of today have to show us the way. If I have failed in my duty as Chair, I am more than willing to step down, but I would urge everyone to remember how often we Gujaratis have been the outsiders and have asked to be accepted in. I speak as a mother when I say that I'm sure that in our hearts what all of us want is for our children to be happy.

Mohan   Hear, hear! Prema *bhen*! I would like to say that as a father I thought I had the God-given right to choose my son's path. I was willing for him to sacrifice his life stacking shelves, when God has given him a talent that I chose to close my eyes to. His mother died in this season and I have carried that wound. When I was attacked recently, I realised the most important thing in life. Someone's son helped me, and there I was allowing my son to disappear before my eyes.

Shanti   Are you sure those boys didn't hit him on the head?

Anant *goes up to* **Mohan**.

Anant   Thank you, Bapu. It was you, wasn't it, who got Raza here?

Mohan   He was already here. Playing squash downstairs. Ready to play Romeo.

Anant   How do you know he was downstairs?

Mohan   Mobiles have their uses. Instant communication. Your grandmother had the number, I just pressed the button.

Anant   Bapu, Julian is keen for me to come on board.

Mohan   With my blessing.

Anant   He wants me to choreograph a dance for Meera Syal.

Mohan   Well, if anyone can give steps to that *gulab jamun* it's you.

Anant   I've told him that if he wants me, he has to shoot in your kiosk.

Mohan   Two birds with one stone. Spoken like a true Patel.

Anant   Come and meet him, Bapu.

Mohan *and* **Anant** *leave.* **Prema** *is back on the tannoy.*

Prema   I'd like everyone to join me in congratulating Preethi and Raza.

General applause as **Prema** *hugs and congratulates* **Raza**.

Preethi   Thank you, Mum.

Roopa *comes and hugs* **Preethi**.

Roopa   Your mum's wicked. Safe.

Preethi   Yeah. She's come good.

Roopa   I'm sorry about your dad.

Preethi   You knew?

Roopa   Everyone knows.

Preethi   And there's you having the hump with me for keeping secrets?

Roopa   Will you say sorry to Jaz for me?

Raza   No worries.

One by one, the youngsters all come and congratulate them. **Bharat** *and* **Popatlal** *also come and grudgingly congratulate them.*

Popatlal   Congratulations, Preethi! Raza! You've crossed over very well. I thought dancing was against your religion.

Raza   No.

Popatlal   No, of course, it's just intoxication that is not permitted.

Raza   Alcohol.

Popatlal   Yes, although it could be argued that a woman's beauty is more intoxicating than a peg of whisky. Prema *bhen*, Pushpa and I would like to take our hats off to you. We have had so much of enjoyment and who would have thought this was the season for both our daughters to meet their matches?

Prema   Who would have thought? So Bharat *bhai*, can the Lohana ladies count on our arrangement for next year's dates?

Bharat   I have not been equitable. I'm going to rotate the hall between the castes. So it will be the Shah turn.

Popatlal   Pushpa is already talking to the Mayor and Mayoress about next season. I hope you don't mind, but imitation is the best form of flattery.

Prema   Not at all . . . I look forward to being a guest rather than host next season!

Popatlal   Most welcome.

Shrenek   Got to hand it to you, Raza. You're a great dancer and you swing a better left hook than me.

Music comes on. **Preethi** *and* **Raza** *start to dance and one by one everyone joins in.*

Printed in the USA
CPSIA information can be obtained
at www.ICGtesting.com
LVHW041102171024
794057LV00001B/214

9 780413 774224